MARTIN LUTHER'S LAST WILL AND TESTAMENT

MARTIN LUTHER'S LAST WILL AND TESTAMENT

A FACSIMILE OF THE ORIGINAL DOCUMENT, WITH AN ACCOUNT OF ITS ORIGINS, COMPOSITION AND SUBSEQUENT HISTORY

BY TIBOR FABINY

Distributed in the U.S.A. by
Humanities Press
Atlantic Highlands, N.J.

USSHER PRESS
DUBLIN

CORVINA KIADÓ
BUDAPEST

Original title:
Luther Márton végrendelete
Corvina Kiadó, Budapest, 1982

Translated by Rudolf Fischer

Design by Ferenc Barabás

Photographs by
Deutsche Fotothek, Dresden: 1, 3, 4, 12, 15, 23–25, 29
Deutsche Staatsbibliothek, Berlin: 20
Lutherhalle, Wittenberg: 5–11, 13, 14, 16–19, 21, 22, 26–28, 30, 31, 33–38
Hungarian National Museum (Photo Zsuzsa Erdőkürti): 32
Universitätsbibliothek der Karl-Marx-Universität, Leipzig: 2

On the cover:
Martin Luther by Lucas Cranach the Elder,
Kurpfälzisches Museum, Heidelberg
Reproduction by János Szerencsés

The Ussher Press is the imprint of The Friends of the Library,
Trinity College, Dublin
ISBN 0–904720–15–2
ISBN 963 13 1582 7

Contents

Introduction

Early on the morning of 18 February 1546, Martin Luther died in Eisleben. The house—it is now over five hundred years old—at 7 Andreaskirchplatz was a handsome building with an upper storey. It had been made available to the great reformer a few weeks earlier by his generous friend and patron, Count Albrecht VII of Mansfeld, through the agency of the tenant Johann Albrecht, the town clerk. Luther's business in Eisleben was to act as arbitrator in a protracted dispute over the patrimony of his former liege lords, the Counts of Mansfeld. Negotiations at Andreaskirchplatz were going well enough to produce a temporary reconciliation between the brothers and cousins Mansfeld on 14 February. But by then Luther's health had been undermined by lingering ailments, the extremely cold winter weather, and the stress to which he had been so recently subjected.

The man who had reshaped the spiritual map of the entire continent of Europe died aged sixty-two in the town of his birth and baptism. (The death-bed is still in place, together with the Mansfeld coat of arms and, above the bed, life-size copies of portraits of Martin and Katharina Luther by Lucas Cranach the Elder.) In attendance at the moment of his death were Count Albrecht of Mansfeld and his wife, Anna, together with Count Johann Heinrich and Countess Margareta of Schwarzburg-Leutenberg, the town clerk and his wife. Two of Luther's assistants, Johann Aurifaber and Ambrosius Rudtfeld, were present also, with Michael Cölius who was court chaplain to the Mansfeld family, Justus Jonas, the reformer from Halle, and finally, two physicians.

Next morning a note in Latin written in Luther's own hand was found on his desk. It read (in English translation):

No one who has not been a shepherd for five years can understand Virgil's Bucolics. No one who has not been a ploughman for five years can understand Virgil's Georgics. No one who has not been active in communal affairs for twenty-five years can understand Cicero's Letters. No one should imagine he really knows the taste of Holy Scripture if he has not guided the church for one hundred years with prophets such as Elijah and Elisha, with John the Baptist, with Christ and His Apostles... We are but beggars. That is the truth. 16 February, 1546.[1]

Philipp Melanchthon's last letter to Martin Luther, dated 18 February (the day of Luther's death) included news of Protestant life in Hungary brought by "an upstanding man, true to his faith".[2] Together with an ointment which Luther had left behind in Wittenberg and which arrived by the same mail, this letter reached Eisleben too late. Nevertheless, this final reference to Lutheranism in Hungary is significant in the context of Luther's will and the subsequent fate of the document. The "upstanding man, true to his faith" was Zsigmond Torda from Gyalu in Transylvania, a former student of Melanchthon's in Wittenberg and later headmaster in Eperjes (today, Prešov in Czechoslovakia). Torda, born in Gyalu some time between 1518 and 1520, attended school at Gyulafehérvár (today, Alba Iulia in Rumania), and went to university first in Cracow and after 1539/40, in Wittenberg. Graduating as Master of Arts in 1544, he returned home to Eperjes in the following year, and became tutor to the sons of Ferenc Révay, the Vice Palatine. Some years later he accompanied his charges to Padua where he continued his studies for a number of years. That journey, however, as well as his return to Eperjes as headmaster, belongs to a period well after Luther's death.

Torda had only been back in Eperjes for a year when Luther died in Eisleben. He had already reported on a number of occasions to his former teacher Melanchthon at Wittenberg on the advance of the Turks and the state of the Reformation in Hungary. Though his early letters had complained repeatedly about the Turkish "yoke", in this last letter he noted that, under the Turks, "the Gospel was freely preached, enjoying widespread circulation," and that even in the Ottoman Empire "there was many a preacher of the word of God, and comforter of prisoners."[3] Melanchthon in his childhood had been tutored by a Hungarian, Johannes Hungarus, and had always felt close to that country. Consequently he was keen to pass Torda's good news on to Luther, bearing in mind as well that Luther had often written on the Turkish question. But by the time the message was delivered, the cortège was already on the road from Saint Andrew's Church, Eisleben, to Wittenberg, by way of Halle.

Luther's last will and testament, made in 1542 to secure the position of his wife Katharina, had been registered by the law officer in Wittenberg, together with a supplementary clause (in 1544) designed to protect its provisions from challenge. Written in Luther's hand, and witnessed by three of his closest associates, Philipp Melanchthon, Caspar Cruciger, and Johannes Bugerhagen, the document is now in the possession of the Lutheran Church of Hungary, and preserved in the National Lutheran Archives in Budapest where, naturally, it is considered as its greatest treasure. The conditions under which it came into being, its substantive content, and its subsequent history, are the subject of this short study published to honour the five-hundredth anniversary of the reformer's birth.

The Marriage in Wittenberg

The year 1525 was decisive both in the history of the German Empire and in Luther's life. The Twelve Articles issued by the Swabian peasants in insurrection, Luther's position in relation to this rising and the pamphlets he wrote on it, Thomas Münzer's decapitation in Thuringia, the butchery of some hundred thousand peasants in Germany—all these events agitated public opinion throughout Europe. And then Frederick the Wise, Elector of Saxony, died. Founder of the University of Wittenberg, and the Pope's candidate as Holy Roman Emperor, Frederick had early recognized Luther's spiritual greatness and accepted the reforming doctrines. In the seven years leading up to his death, he had been instrumental in spreading the Reformation as its first great patron in the central area of the Empire. Given this sombre background of national suffering and the Elector's death, we might be excused for passing over the celebration of Luther's marriage.

Twenty years had passed since he had entered the Augustinian monastery at Erfurt as a twenty-one year-old novice. His parents, Hans and Margaretha[4], had been distressed by this decision, and they remained so even after his decision in 1517 to confront Pope and Emperor for his conscience's sake. In October 1524 Luther finally put aside his friar's habit, but continued to observe his vows. He had for many years, in letters, sermons and six writings specifically on marriage, family life, priestly celibacy, and clerical vows, praised marriage as a goodly estate instituted by God and confirmed by Christ, a most honourable state to which priests had belonged for over a thousand years, like prophets and apostles before them, unless some inner need had urged voluntary vows of chastity on them.

In his commentary on *1 Corinthians 7,* Luther argued that chastity is certainly "a merry, comely and fine talent for those who have it," but exceedingly rare, since few, "barely one in a thousand", are born with it. Those who did possess it were "God's special miracles" who, doing without marriage, neither "suffered rut" nor took refuge in concubinage. All who were not among these rare exceptions should stay true to their congenital nature and take a wife, just as they took meat for their hunger and drink for their thirst. In his 1520 *An den christlichen Adel deutscher Nation* (Address to the Christian Nobility of the German Nation), he denounced the Papacy which, by prescribing priestly celibacy, had plunged the clergy into the moral depravity of a widespread concubinage. A Council was required, he wrote, to allow once again "freedom to enter the married state". Young candidates for the priesthood were advised not to take vows of celibacy on ordination until some such change had taken place.

If it appears from this that Luther had already intellectually and morally mastered the arguments in favour of the holy state of matrimony, it is nonetheless clear that in 1521 he had no personal motives for doing so. Looking back to the Diet of Worms of that year, he declared on a later occasion that he would have laughed outright at any suggestion that, within a few years, he would be a husband and even a father. In 1521 he had written from the Wartburg to Spalatin: "Good Lord, the good people of Wittenberg will end up providing wives for the monks, but they will not be able to force one on me." Six and a half months before his wedding he was still writing to Spalatin that

> *the way my heart felt up to now, and still feels, it is unlikely that I will take a wife. Not that I am unaware of my flesh or sex, since I am not made of either wood or stone; but my mind is far from marriage, since I daily expect death and the well-deserved punishment of an heretic. That is why I neither wish to set up a target for God in what He intends with me, nor fix upon anything in my heart; but I hope He will not let me live much longer.*[5]

Soon, however, this same expectation of death was transformed from an obstacle to marriage into a motive for marriage, and in due course Luther the married man discovered many more unsuspected advantages in marriage that were particularly useful for a clergyman. Earlier, a monastery had seemed the most suitable place for the service to which the Lord had called him: later it was to be the family hearth. All the troubles and burdens of a household, and of the upbringing of children, which Luther had avoided in the past for the sake of higher objectives, turned out to be character-building duties.

The third period of his life produced a new recognition in him that certain virtues, like a readiness for self-sacrifice, renunciation, forgiveness, and reconciliation, could only be properly practised within marriage.

Who, then, was Luther about to marry? In 1509 Katharina von Bora had been taken as a ten-year-old novice to the Cistercian Convent at Nimbschen near Grimma—today in ruins. It has been maintained that this daughter of an impoverished noble family had earlier been sent to the Benedictine convent at Brehna near Bitterfeld, at the age of five. When she finally took her vows in 1513 Nimbschen held forty-three nuns in all, including an aunt of hers. In the years following, Luther's writings were spreading like wildfire. Early in the 1520s Nimbschen (like many other places) found itself in uproar, the more so since the parish priest himself supported the radical wing of the Reformation. *De votis monasticis* (Concerning Monastic Vows, 1521), a sermon *Vom ehelichen Leben* (On Married Life, 1522), and then the explosive epistle *Ursache und Antwort dass Jungfrauen Klöster göttlich verlassen können* (Cause and Response that Maidens may Leave Convents in a Godly State, 1523) found the greatest response from monks, friars, and nuns.

On Easter Eve, 4 April 1523, twelve nuns, including Katharina von Bora, escaped from Nimbschen with the help of three burghers from Torgau. One of the three was Alderman Leonhard Koppe, victualler to the priory, whose cart attracted no suspicion in the vicinity of the priory. The twelve girls slipped out through a gap cut in the mud wall and hid under Koppe's tarpaulin. The story of noble maidens escaping in herring barrels may be discounted, for there is no word of this in the Torgau Chronicle for 1523 which states quite clearly that the cart which took the girls to Wittenberg via Torgau was otherwise empty. Three of the twelve were sheltered by relatives in the Saxon Electorate and these travelled only as far as Torgau. The nine who travelled on to Wittenberg did so because their homes were in that other part of Saxony ruled by Luther's sworn enemy, Duke George. The whole affair was enough of an adventure to raise eyebrows even in so staunch a stronghold of the Reformation as Wittenberg. The eminent citizens who alternated as burgomaster were, however, solidly allied to Luther who could count also on the support of his liege lord Frederick the Wise.

In 1523 the ruling burgomaster was Lucas Cranach the Elder, one of the most famous painters of his time. He was also the owner of a pharmacy, a printing workshop, and a wine-cellar, all located in his house on the Market Square in Wittenberg. From the outset he took charge of Katharina von Bora with almost parental solicitude—she was at the time twenty-four years old. Cranach and his wife Barbara found lodgings for their new charge with the recently appointed town clerk, Philipp Reichenbach. His family home was a few minutes' walk from the Cranach's, in a street behind the town church, where Katharina proved most helpful in receiving and attending on guests. It is a further mark of the eminence of these abettors of fugitive nuns that Magister Reichenbach became burgomaster himself in 1530.

The closeness and social consequence of these circles had its importance for Luther's personal life. Katharina von Bora often visited him in the Black Convent (where he lived), for he had concerned himself for the future of the nine "convent maidens" who had arrived in Wittenberg. She also called on Philipp Melanchthon whose wife was the daughter of former burgomaster Krapp. In the Melanchthon home she met Hieronymus Baumgartner, a young patrician from Nuremberg. In the course of this visit to old university friends, Baumgartner seemed to establish some understanding with Katharina and the two seemed to be in love. Nevertheless, he returned home single and subsequently he married the daughter of a wealthy family. Martin Luther, who knew of Katharina's disappointment, thought he could best serve her by marrying her off. In his *Table Talk,* some fourteen years later, he confessed that, had he wished to marry in 1524 he would have chosen another of the Nimbschen nuns (the attractive Ave von Schönfeld from Magdeburg) or—as Pastor Nikolaus von Amsdorf suggested—Ave Alemann.[6]

Spring 1525 brought a change in these relations. Katharina complained to Amsdorf that Luther wanted to marry her off against her wishes. In speaking to the Magdeburg pastor she made it clear that she had no objection to marriage as such, and that she would accept an offer from a man like Luther or Amsdorf himself. The latter (a settled bachelor) passed the message to Luther who was in fact contemplating marriage by this time. However, he had thought Katharina to be arrogant—wrongly thought so, as he confessed later in his *Table Talk*. Resolving to "spite the devil", he visited the Cranach and Reichenbach homes with increasing frequency. Much gossip ensued, even among university circles. Melanchthon, who was Luther's closest friend and collaborator, warned him most emphatically of the consequences of tittle-tattle to the entire cause of the Reformation and the achievements of seven years' hard work. For some weeks Luther avoided the topic by avoiding Melanchthon. Then suddenly he decided to marry Katharina von Bora and to marry her on 13 June 1525.

That date (13 June) is still celebrated in the Roman Church as the feast of Saint Anthony of Padua. In 1525 that date fell on a Tuesday, the day of the week which is specifically under the protection of Saint Anthony—it was indeed the first Tuesday after Trinity Sunday. Since Saint Anthony of Padua is the patron saint of marriage, one may conclude that Luther chose the date for his marriage with particular care. Given this attention to significant detail in the church calendar, and given also the carnage of the peasant insurrection and its brutal suppression in the vicinity of Wittenberg, it is useful to inquire further into questions of canon law for some further explanation of this decision by an Augustinian friar and a Cistercian nun.

By the custom of the time, a marriage took place in two stages. The first, the *copula carnalis,* was a brief ceremony preceded by an oral agreement *(concensus)* between the two persons about to be married. Laymen were acceptable as witnesses at this stage, and even the agent *(fungens)* was not necessarily a clerk in holy orders. Having asked for and received the agreement of bride and bridegroom, the *fungens* then declared them man and wife and the witnesses took the couple to the symbolic nuptial couch—hence *copula carnalis,* a symbolic consummation of marriage. It was this ceremony which Luther asked his father confessor, friend and colleague, Johann Bugenhagen to perform on the evening of 13 June. The witnesses were: Justus Jonas (prior of All Hallows and a fellow teacher at the University), Johann Apel (professor of canon law and a former canon of Würzburg—who had spent three months in the bishop of Bamberg's gaol for the offence of marrying a nun), Lucas Cranach the Elder, and Cranach's wife Barbara. Apel drafted the marriage contract, and the ceremony took place in the Black Convent which had been given to Luther by Frederick the Wise after Brisger, the last Augustinian prior in Wittenberg, had left. We have three authentic contemporary sources for these details: separate reports by Georg Spalatin and Johann Bugenhagen and, in addition, a letter full of anxiety and consternation written by Melanchthon to his friend the Protestant humanist Joachim Camerarius (1500–1574), who reorganized the University of Leipzig.

The second stage, the wedding breakfast, still lay ahead. According to sixteenth-century custom, that had to take place either the following morning or, at least, within a few days of the *copula carnalis*. In pre-Tridentine days, this was not an office of the church sanctioned by canon law, but involved attendance at an early mass where the couple were blessed by the parish priest in the presence of friends and relatives. Since Luther had decided on marriage too suddenly to allow for notification of his parents and family, the second stage of the marriage only took place on 27 June, a full fortnight later and so also on a Tuesday. In addition to his parents and close relatives, Luther included among his invited friends Amsdorf, Koppe, and Spalatin.

Though the majority of teachers there disapproved, the University of Wittenberg presented the young couple with a magnificent silver cup which today is preserved in Greifswald. The Town Council provided vintage wine, a firkin of Einbeck beer, and twenty guilders in silver coin. A greater surprise came in the form of twenty gold guilders sent by Albrecht von Brandenburg through the agency of Johann Rühel, counsellor of the Counts of Mansfeld and one of Luther's friends. As Elector of Mainz, Albrecht of Brandenburg was a beneficiary of that sale of indulgences which Luther had opposed since 1517, and as archbishop of Mainz he was involved in the trade himself. Luther therefore refused these gold guilders for his own part, though he left Katharina free to accept them if she should so choose. On Rühel's advice, she accepted Albrecht's gift.

Most of those intellectually close to Luther celebrated with him, happy that the man who had taught "with letters and words" had now sealed his teaching with a bold deed worthy of the Reformation. The letter to Camerarius referred to above suggests that Melanchthon at first felt injured, or rather anxious, wondering whether the marriage might damage Luther's reputation at a time when Germany needed all his strength. Erasmus of Rotterdam, in common with the Wittenberg gossips, suspected at first that pregnancy had prompted the couple to their decision, but he quickly withdrew any such imputation.

A far more complex motivation, linking political and theological issues, lay at the heart of the matter. There is every evidence that Luther, who had been placed under the imperial ban some years earlier, seriously reckoned with the possibility of arrest and a martyr's death. The enforcement of the law against heresy had, after all, been confirmed once again at the Diet of Nuremberg in April 1524. And already in 1522 Luther declared that, as Satan had attacked his fold, he "owed it to them to suffer death for them. I will do that gladly and happily, by God's grace..." Time was pressing if he were still "to make the angels laugh and the demons cry," as he wrote to Spalatin on 16 June.[7] Ten days before the *copula carnalis* he wrote to Rühel,

> *since I am minded, before I should leave this life, to enter the married estate, which I respect as demanded by God, though it be no more than a betrothal like Joseph's...*[8]

Two days after the first stage of the marriage ceremonies, he wrote again to Rühel and reiterated the connection between his marriage and his relations with the authorities ecclesiastical and political:

> *Now lords and priests and peasants are all against me, and threaten me with death. All right, since they are mad and foolish, I will also hurry up to find myself at my end in an estate created by God, retaining nothing of my earlier Popish life about me, to make them madder and more foolish still as best I can, and then goodbye...*[9]

The married estate, therefore, was of vital importance as a deed, teaching by example a conviction firmly held. Luther records his spiritual concern that he should not die before entering a state demanded by God. Should something befall him between the *copula carnalis* and the wedding breakfast, this state would remain "a betrothal like Joseph's", but that was not truly his aim. Though he married as a reformer, he took a wife as a man, who was "neither wood nor stone".

Poverty and Riches

Luther's marriage to Katharina von Bora naturally came to affect the manner in which he ultimately might dispose of his worldly property; however, the influence of his family circumstances in the broader sense—together with the complications of the domestic economy—cannot be set aside. The elder Luthers are known to posterity through Cranach's portraits: Hans Luther, a former miner, was an alderman and householder of Mansfeld when he died early in May 1530 shortly after the great Diet of Augsburg; his wife, who survived him by a year, died in Eisleben in the summer of 1531. Martin Luther's own family consisted of six children, one of whom died in infancy and another at the age of thirteen. His experience of parenthood naturally affected his view of matrimony, and some consideration of his children should preface our study of his last will and testament.

The first child, Johann, was born on 7 June 1526 in Wittenberg, and died in Königsberg in 1575 aged 49 by which time he had achieved the rank of Court Councillor. In 1553 (after his father's death) he married Elizabeth, daughter of the Wittenberg scholar Caspar Cruciger, a friend of Luther's active in Magdeburg and Leipzig. The second child, Elizabeth, died at the age of eight months in August 1528. Magdalena was born on 4 May 1529 and died on 20 September 1542. The letters in which the father recorded his conversations and prayers at her death-bed still constitute a moving portion of Lutheran devotional reading.

Martin Luther the Younger was born on 7 November 1531. Though he completed a theological course, poor health prevented him from entering the service of the church. He married Anna Heilinger, daughter of a burgomaster, and he lived on private means in Wittenberg where he died childless in 1565. The fifth child, Paul, lived longest: born in 1533, he studied medicine and became a respected court physician successively at Gotha, Brandenburg, and

Dresden. He died in Leipzig in 1593. One of his six children, Johann Ernst, entered the Church, like his grandfather, becoming provost of the cathedral chapter of Zeitz. Luther's youngest child, Margarete, was born on 17 December 1534 and died in Mühlhausen (Prussia) in 1570, the wife of Georg von Kunheim, a Prussian nobleman.

Luther, at home, spoke of himself as a happy man blessed with riches, and his family were central to this contentment. Paul had not yet been born when he said at table:

> *I have every reason to be content, I have three legitimate children, something no Popish theologian can boast of, and the three children are three kingdoms, who are my own by better inheritance than Ferdinand's Hungary, Bohemia, and the Holy Roman realm.*[10]

Apart from his children, many others lived in Luther's household. First among these was Katharina von Bora's aunt who had fled from Nimbschen shortly after the escape of the twelve. Luther had had rooms in the Black Convent furnished specially for her, and she made herself useful especially in looking after the children. She died in 1537. In addition were numerous nieces and nephews whose entry into adult life Luther had to supervise. Two nieces and a grandniece, with two nephews (Hans Polner and Cyriak Kaufmann), formed the centre of this group which included younger and older students who took their meals in the Luther household. These latter included Matthias of Déva, a prominent member of the first generation of reformers in Hungary.

Konrad Cordatus, an Austrian reformer active in Hungary, was the first (in 1531) to record Luther's table talk. It is he who perhaps tells us most of Luther's comments over twenty years on his beloved and loyal wife. A year after their marriage, he declared "I would not exchange my Kate for France, not even if Venice were added."[11] And eleven years later, "I have fared well, God be praised, for I have a pious and loyal wife, on whom her husband's heart may rely, as Solomon says, 'she spoils nothing for me'."[12] Blending a little German to good effect with Latin, Luther lets us know how fully his wife needed time and strength to carry out all her domestic duties:

Lord Kate, who carries, ploughs the fields, herds and buys and sells cattle, brews etc. salutes you. Furthermore she has tackled the Bible since I promised her 50 guilders if she finished before Easter. There is much seriousness. She has already reached Deuteronomy.[13]

Katharina Luther, on whom whole pages of pet-names might be bestowed—"My Kate... my rib... my Lord and Moses Kate... my morning star of Wittenberg"—was admirably suited to the arduous management of Luther's house and estate. She arranged for a cellar to be added, as well as the building of pigsties; she transformed the convent's graveyard into a fertile kitchen garden, and leased fields that she might farm them. She also bought her brother's estate at Zülsdorf near Kieritzsch, between Leipzig and Borna, a decision of considerable importance later in connection with her husband's last will.

Nevertheless, the Luther family was far from wealthy. For, against the new properties and the accumulating gifts one must set the very substantial household expenses of the reformer and his extensive family. Certainly, Luther cannot be said to have been keen on amassing worldly goods. "Wealth is the smallest thing on earth, and the smallest gift that God can give a man..." And again, "Where there is much there are also a great many sins."[14]

Justus Jonas is only one of the several witnesses to Luther's belief, after a serious attack of asthenia in July 1527, that he would soon die. Having confessed and received absolution from Bugenhagen, he asked that his son Hans be brought to his bedside. He blessed the boy and said: "Now I commend my dearest Kate and you to my dear and gracious God. You have no one but God, who is a father to orphans and judge of widows, and will surely nourish and take care of you." Then he referred his wife to the sole legacy he could leave to her, some silver cups, adding that "you know we have nothing, except them."[15] Some time later he commented, "I keep a very odd household; I consume more than my income. I need 500 guilders every year for housekeeping, for the kitchen, not to mention clothes, other utensils and charity, and my annual stipend is only 200 guilders."[16] (By comparison, in 1518 Melanchthon was paid one hundred guilders a year by the University of Wittenberg, and 400 guilders in 1560; on the other hand, a cow cost three guilders, a goat or calf cost two, and a pig one—the "Haus Bruno," which Luther bought in Wittenberg, cost 400 guilders.)

Any estimate of the Luthers' financial circumstances must take into account primarily their acquisition of property. At the time of their marriage neither had any. The wedding presents constituted their first possessions of value. Difficult years followed in which they often lacked even fuel to heat their large house. The house, formerly the Black Convent, was allotted to them by Frederick the Wise as a dwelling in a transfer which had to be carried out surreptitiously since the town of Wittenberg itself had some claim at least on the attached lands, sheds, and so forth. Luther was given the dwelling for his own use, tax-free for life. The deed of gift was subsequently confirmed by Frederick's successors, and included a licence to brew beer on the usual twelve occasions each year.

The former convent, known as Collegium Augusteum after 1546, and including the building now called the Lutherhalle, was only two thirds its later size when Luther took it over. It still required considerable sums to be spent on it to satisfy the needs of all who dwelt there. From accounts in Luther's own hand we know that by Easter 1542 he had laid out 1,805 guilders in all, in a brewery and brewing implements, stabling for horses, cowsheds and pigsties, gate-lodges, a bathroom, washtubs, cellars, additional rooms, chimneys, a staircase, a garden and well, a vestibule, and a roof. The "Katharinenportal" which served as an entrance was built by Katharina Luther in 1539, complete with two benches on either side. A half-length picture of her husband was placed over one, and his rose-seal over the other, both carved in sandstone from Pirna on the Elbe.

At the time of Luther's illness in July 1527 (as in the will composed fifteen years later) there is no mention of the Black Convent property. The deed of gift had included a clause establishing the donor's right of pre-emption by which the Elector maintained a right to buy back his gift and by which the property might not be passed on to a third party. Luther's heirs did indeed sell the property to the Elector August I of Saxony in 1564 (for three thousand and seven hundred guilders), and the Elector put it at the University's disposal as the Collegium Augusteum. Prior to that transference, in 1535 Luther's property was extended by the purchase of a small garden (probably the hop garden) for twenty guilders, and a larger garden (probably the orchard), for nine hundred guilders. In the autumn of the same year he paid ninety guilders each for a field and an adjoining garden.

Given the conditions on which Luther acquired the Black Convent it was bound to play a lesser part in the story of his last will and testament than those other properties he subsequently acquired. In 1540 he paid six hundred and ten guilders to his needy brother-in-law Hans von Bora for his estate, Zülsdorf (Zollsdorf in older documents). At the same time he assisted Hans von Bora to become steward of the Benedictine house in Leipzig. In this way, though the estate promised little profit, the "inherited roof" did not fall into the hands of strangers. In addition, Katharina Luther was very ill in 1540 and in need of a quiet retreat in which to recover from a miscarriage.

In the summer of that year Luther was already addressing his wife as "My gracious lady, Katherin Luther of Bora and Zülsdorf near Wittenberg, my love." In another letter from the same period he wrote to "the wealthy lady of Zülsdorf, Katherin Luther, wife of Doctor Luther, bodily resident at Wittenberg, spiritually ambling in Zülsdorf, my love." To Spalatin he wrote proudly and jocularly that everything needed would be obtained *"ut reginam nouam in regnum suum statuamus"* (that the new queen be installed in her realm).[17] Once Katharina was back on her feet, she set to work to restore the Zülsdorf estate. In this the Luthers were assisted by a gift from the Elector John Frederick: at the outset he gave the new owners six hundred guilders towards the restoration, and on two subsequent occasions presented them with timber for new stables and a barn from the Altenburg forest.

Within a few years Zülsdorf became a second home, a refuge for Martin and Katharina Luther from the disputes of Wittenberg. On 28 June 1545 he wrote to her:

> *I would love to arrange it that I might not return to Wittenberg. My heart has grown cold, and I no longer like being there. I wish you would sell the garden and plot, house and farmyard, and I would give back the large house to My Gracious Lord, and it would be best for you if you settled in Zülsdorf while I still lived, and I could help you with my stipend to improve the estate.*[18]

He seemed to have a premonition of death and wished to see his widow safe from those "four elements" (of which below) which after his death would neither spare Katharina nor tolerate her in Wittenberg —"it would be better done in my lifetime, what will have to be done." In all his later letters, including the last letter from Eisleben, addressed to his "dearly beloved housewife Katherin Luther, doctor's wife, of Zülsdorf and Wittenberg," he gives precedence to Zülsdorf over Wittenberg.

One final piece of property still awaits discussion, Haus Bruno, which Luther bought in 1541. This had belonged to Eberhard Brisger, the last Augustinian prior in Wittenberg, who married a local girl in July 1525. The Wittenbergers took exception to this step and at the express wish of Luther and Elector John the Steadfast Brisger moved to Altenburg. After some time the house was sold to Bruno Brauer who in due course found himself in financial difficulties and who offered the property to Luther for four hundred and twenty guilders. Luther was only able to raise a deposit of one hundred and twenty guilders, and paid the rest in twelve instalments, the first at Whitsun 1543 and the last falling due in 1554. The small and narrow building (long since demolished) looks quite modest in the sole surviving engraving. And yet the interior was sufficiently impressive to include a bathroom, as listed in the contract of sale.[19]

Luther's second and last will shows that he meant the house for his widow and children, and several letters support this intention. He often complained of the huge expenses of the Black Convent: the "large house" was in a state of disrepair and demanded more maintenance than a husbandless family could have coped with. On the other hand Luther feared that the Convent might suffer damage by being incorporated in the fortifications in preparations for war. "That is why I thought to anticipate that by buying the nearest space to it, Haus Bruno, for 400 and 20 guilders," he wrote on 26 March 1542 to the Elector John Frederick the Magnanimous. In the event, the Schmalkadic War only broke out in 1546, after Luther's death. The Black Convent, however, remained the property of Luther's sons longer even than the Haus Bruno which they sold in 1557 for three hundred thalers.

Luther Plagued by Illness

From the many portraits of Luther which we possess—most of them the work of Lucas Cranach the Elder—we would gather that he enjoyed robust good health. Yet the vitality of his appearance concealed physical weakness, and his extraordinary achievements make one forget the many ailments from which he suffered. Stomach and kidney trouble, harbingers of more serious later illness, were probably the result of his years as a monk at Erfurt, his strict fasting and extended mortification on the damp floor of his cell. He was often plagued by violent headaches, lasting for weeks, accompanied by a buzzing in the ear and vertigo. At times like these, light hurt his eyes and he found himself unable to read or write for extended periods of days or weeks. In 1526 the first symptoms of kidney stones were noticed.

These medical complications naturally enough had their bearing upon the circumstances of the composition of his will and on the circumstances of his death. A fontanel resulting from a leg abcess in 1532 had seemed to offer relief for certain problems of the circulation: in 1543, therefore, it was decided in keeping with the practice of the time to keep the humours flowing artificially, and the salve or ointment which Luther requested in his last letter from Eisleben was required for this purpose.

Luther compiled his *Geistiges Gesangbüchlein* (Little Hymnbook) in 1524, daily expecting arrest and death at the stake. It consists of twenty-four hymns, some his own compositions, some versions of earlier hymns including a version of the well-known medieval lament *"Mitten wir im Leben sind mit dem Tod umfangen"* (In the midst of life we are surrounded by death) rendered as *"Mitten in dem Tode wir im Leben stehn"* (In the midst of death we are in life). In 1519 the *Sermon von der Bereitung zum Sterben* (Sermon on the Preparation for Death) advised: "Do not look on hell with predestination either in yourself or in itself; but look at the divine image, Christ, who was abandoned by God for your sake, as if he were damned for all eternity; in *that* image your hell is overcome."

These are the words of one firmly rooted in his faith, one who knew how to despise his own suffering. Thus, one day at table, having been constipated for some time, he said that one's rump deserved its due—he was quite unlike those scholars who forgot the most essential things when they were writing or reading. Luther did not allow illness to sap his energy. Work was sustained even on days of serious incapacity. One zealous scholar calculated that, in 1521 when Luther was ill for seven months, he was the author of thirty publications and one hundred letters, he wrote and delivered seventy sermons. Ill for ten months in 1545, he still produced thirteen publications, eighty letters and thirty-five sermons. It was as if suffering inwardly steeled his will.

Luther's serious illness at Schmalkalden is particularly important for our present purposes, since it took him close to death and prompted him to make his will. He had joined the meeting of allied Protestants in February 1537. At Elector John Frederick's behest he had drafted what have come to be known as the Schmalkaldic Articles as a basis for discussion in the face of two papal bulls directed precisely against the "pestilential Lutheran" heresy. The Schmalkaldic League—seven North German principalities and eleven free imperial cities—sought to find in the Articles a common platform for the forthcoming Council. Most of the members had brought their theologians—indeed John Frederick had come with Luther, Bugenhagen, Melanchthon, and Spalatin—and around forty of them assembled in Schmalkalden by 7 February 1537, in addition to the military party. In the first few days no meetings were held, but Luther (despite his illness) preached three sermons. By early January he had been already confined to bed with kidney trouble, though this had not prevented him from completing the Articles and discussing them with Melanchthon, Bugenhagen, Cruciger, Jonas, Amsdorf, Spalatin, and Agricola.

The room at the inn where Luther slept was musty, the bed-linen damp and cold. He was not used to the spicy food and found the bread too doughy. His condition visibly deteriorated until he was unable to get out of bed to attend the conferences. The Articles which have since been accepted as a definition of Lutheranism were not submitted to the estates in his absence, but only signed by the theologians present, and that after the meeting had formally risen. This was all the more painful for Luther since the Papal Nuncio, who noticed he was missing from the sessions, unavoidably discovered that he was ill. By the second half of February his illness reached a critical stage, including repeated bouts of renal colic, urinary obstruction, diarrhea and vomiting. The doctors were helpless; there was no pharmacy in Schmalkalden.

On 26 February the journey home began with two carriages provided by the Elector. The first, fitted out with a bed, was occupied by Luther himself and five companions, including a physician, Georg Sturz from Erfurt. The second contained a charcoal fire in a brazier on which food was prepared and all sorts of implements for keeping the patient warm. The first night, at Tambach in Thuringia, produced a sudden, unexpected, but temporary improvement in Luther's condition. After eight days he was at last able to pass water. Luther wrote to Melanchthon in that hour of relief: "The father of mercy and God of all consolation has taken pity on your prayers and tears in this second hour of the night unexpectedly opening a passage for me... May this example teach us to pray and dare, and to hope for help from heaven..."[20] To his wife he wrote: "Thank God, and let the dear little ones with Aunt Lene thank the true Father, for you surely would have lost this one... God has performed a miracle on me this night, and he does it still thanks to the prayers of the pious."[21]

But on the road from Tambach to Gotha, Luther suffered a more serious attack than ever before. Not expecting to reach Gotha alive, he made an oral declaration of his last will and testament to Bugenhagen in the moving carriage. Luther's first testament, dictated in feverish anticipation of the Papal Council and in extreme physical distress, was copied by Bugenhagen for the Elector John Frederick on his arrival in Gotha, and headed *"Confessio et testamentum venerandi patris nostri D. Lutheri".*

The most striking feature of this first will is that Luther, fifty-three at the time, was not really thinking of death but of the life of the Church. The first sentence announces his resolution in reform, having "stormed against" the Papacy with an altogether clear conscience, since the latter, in all its deeds, blasphemed against Christ and the Gospel. In the second sentence he asks the forgiveness of his chief collaborators—Melanchthon, Jonas, and Cruciger—if he had offended them. The following four sentences speak words of consolation to his wife, and finally commend her and the children to the care of John Frederick and their friends.

Unlike the second will, the great testament of 1542, this document contains only these few lines about the family, and is otherwise entirely devoted to the fate of the Church. He encouraged the Elector of Saxony and the Landgrave of Hessen not to be daunted by calumny, even if they were called spoilators of the Church. "I do not prescribe them manner and measure. May merciful God strengthen them, so they persist with the pure teaching and thank Him for having saved them from the Antichrist." And after some further militant and harsh words against the Papacy, the will recorded by Bugenhagen and preserved today in the State Archives of Weimar closes:

> Post haec commendo animam meam manibus patris et Domini mei Iesu Christi, quem praedicavi et super terram confessus sum.[22]
> *(After this I commend my soul into the hands of the Father and of my Lord Jesus Christ, whom I have preached and confessed on earth.)*

An Irregular Will

Luther recovered. Though on reaching Gotha he actually ordered a tombstone, on 1 March he passed six kidney stones, one of them allegedly as large as a bean. From this point, he began to feel confident that this relief would be a lasting one. Years of hard work followed when earlier complaints manifested themselves comparatively rarely. New works continued to appear, especially sermons and exegeses, a new edition of *Unterricht der Visitatoren* (Instruction of the Visitors, 1538), hymns, and a major work which he had, so to speak, promised in what is called his first will, *Von den Konziliis und Kirchen* (Of Councils and Churches, 1539).

The year 1541 began for Luther with a severe cold, degenerating into various kinds of inflammations. In the spring, at the time of the Diet of Regensburg where the religious question was on the agenda, he was handicapped by ear and eye trouble, headaches and vertigo, to such a degree that he was even unable to pay attention to Melanchthon's reports from Regensburg. For weeks he could neither write by day nor sleep by night. Once again he faced death. This renewed attack was very likely one of the reasons which prompted Luther to draw up his second, great, last will and testament in January 1542.

Since he had dictated the Gotha will five years earlier, Luther's estate had been augmented by the acquisition of Zülsdorf in 1540 and the Haus Bruno in Wittenberg in 1541, not to mention a considerable extension of farming, fruit-growing, gardening, fish-breeding, cattle-raising, and bee-keeping. Prior to becoming a man of property, Luther had experienced the business of making a will as another final opportunity to identify himself with his life as a reformer. He had been of that mind in 1537 at Gotha, and even in 1539 when he referred to Melanchthon's will he declared:

I have nothing to make a will for. My books are available, I leave them to my children; let them become aware that they are no cleverer than their fathers. I declare you, Kate, to be the sole heir. You have borne the children and suckled them. You will not manage their business to their disadvantage. I am opposed to guardians, they seldom do things well.[23]

Thus, at least two years before his 1541 illness, Luther had decided to make provision in time for his wife, so that she "would not have to leave the house like a servant" if he died, or else be wholly dependent on her children or their guardians. Such a decision, however, lacked any foundation in law, though Luther nonetheless managed to carry it into practice successfully.

The *Sachsenspiegel,* a thirteenth-century code of law, the oldest and most influential of its kind in medieval Germany, was still valid in Luther's Saxony. According to the *Sachsenspiegel,* the widow's share of an estate was limited to the *Morgengabe* (a dowry given by the bridegroom the morning after the wedding) and her most personal property such as her clothes and jewels. The estate unconditionally devolved on the child or children, the husband's closest kin being heirs in the absence of any children. The most a man could do in disposing his estate under the laws of Saxony was to secure an annuity on the estate for his widow and even that required the observation of certain formalities.

The alternative, customary for family or testatory arrangements, was Canon Law—which was out of the question for Luther from the start. As an outlawed and excommunicated ex-monk, Luther could not have figured as a lawful testator, nor could his wife (a lapsed nun) have been a lawful heir. Roman Law perhaps offered a third way forward with better prospects of success. This involved Luther making a gift to his wife of all his goods and chattels and installing her as mistress and steward over them, in other words not describing himself as a testator in the first place and renouncing all use of the notion of "widowhood" which was in this instance contestable. In practice, Luther chose this third way, but in doing so he did not employ any of the accepted concepts of donation in Roman Law, but instead cited *Begabung und Leibgedinge* (gift and maintenance). This solution not only promised the best prospects of success but was also most in accord with the views on marriage held by Luther and the Reformation. Thus he not only made a gift in his lifetime of all his goods and chattels to his wife Kate, but also appointed her guardian of his children in the event of his death. In this latter provision, he once again distanced himself from the chosen competence of Roman Law, since it transformed a donation into a testament, one which was irregular in several respects.

By a decree of the Emperor Maximilian I in 1512, a last will and testament, to be legally valid, either had to be drafted by a notary public or at least officially confirmed and signed, sealed and delivered by seven specially chosen witnesses. Luther had studied law at Erfurt and so was competent to draft a deed of gift, with all its appendages, without the help of notary or witness—he distrusted lawyers as a dishonest lot in any case. The efficacy of his will would ultimately depend on the Elector's grace and favour, for which God rather than human witnesses provided a guarantee. Calling himself "God's notary and witness to His gospel", Luther persisted, against all human law, canon or civil, in treating God's word as the only possible legal basis for his will. He thus commended it to Elector John Frederick the Magnanimous, asking "His Electoral Grace... to protect and implement this gift and maintenance graciously."[24] This dispensing with legal formalities only occurs where they run counter to Luther's intentions. Wherever feasible he stuck to the given and acceptable forms of legal procedure. On 11 April 1546, after Luther's death, John Frederick confirmed the document as a valid will and testament.

What follows is the text of Luther's holograph last will and testament, dated Epiphany 1542, and bearing the signatures of Philipp Melanchthon, Caspar Cruciger and Johann Bugenhagen as witnesses, first in German in Luther's wording and spelling, and then in English translation.

Luther's wording

> *Ich Martinus Lüther Doctor e[t]c bekenne mit dieser meiner eigen Handschrifft das ich meiner lieben vnd trewen Hausfrawen Katherin gegeben habe züm leibgedinge (oder wie man das nennen kan) aüff yhr lebelang, damit sie yhres gefallens vnd zü ihrem besten gebaren müge. Vnd gebe yhr das ynn krafft dieses brieües, gegenwertiges vnd heütiges tages*
>
> *Nemlich, das gütlin Zülstorff, wie ich das selb gekaüfft vnd zügericht habe, aller dinge, wie ichs bis daher gehabt habe,*
>
> *Züm andern das Haüs Brüno zur wonüng, so ich vnter meins Wolffs namen gekaüfft habe*

Züm dritten, die Becher vnd kleinot, als ringe, ketten, Schenck groschen, gülden vnd silbern, welche vngeferlich solten bey taüsent gülden werd sein

Das thü ich darümb

Erstlich, das sie mich als ein from, trew, ehlich gemalh, allzeit lieb, werd vnd schon gehalten. Vnd mir dürch reichen Gottes segen fünff lebendige Kinder (die noch für handen, Gott gebe lange) geborn vnd erzogen hat

Züm andern, das sie die Schüld, so ich noch schüldig bin (wo ich sie nicht bey leben ablege) aüff sich nemen vnd bezalen sol, Welcher mag sein ongefer mir bewüst ccccl fl. Mügen sich villeicht wol mehr finden

Züm dritten vnd aller meist darümb, das ich will sie müsst nicht den Kindern, sondern die Kinder sollen yhr ynn die hende sehen, sie ynn ehren halten vnd vnterworffen sein, wie Gott geboten hat. Denn ich wol gesehen vnd erfaren, wie der Teüffel wider die gebot die kinder hetzet vnd reitzet, wenn sie gleich from sind, dürch bose vnd neidissche Meüler sonderlich wenn die müttere widwen sind, Vnd die Söne ehefrawen und die töchtere ehemenner kriegen, vnd widerumb Socrüs Nürüm Nürüs Socrüm.

Denn ich halt, das die Mütter werde yhrer eigen Kinder der beste fürmünde sein, vnd solch gütlin vnd leibgedinge nicht zü der Kinder schaden oder nachteil, sondern zü nütz vnd besserüng braüchen, als die yhr fleisch vnd blüt sind vnd sie vnter yhrem hertzen getragen hat.

Vnd ob sie nach meinem tode, genottigt oder sonst verürsacht würde (denn ich Gott ynn seinen wercken vnd willen, kein Zil setzen kan) sich zu verendern, so trawe ich doch vnd wil hiemit solchs vertrawet haben, sie werde sich mütterlich gegen vnser beider kinder halten. Vnd alles trewlich, es sey leibgedinge oder anders, wie recht ist, mit yhnen teilen

Vnd bitte aüch hiemit vntertheniglich meinen gnedigsten herrn Hertzog Johans Fridrichen Kürfürsten e[t]c s[einer] k[uer] f[ürstlichen] g[naden] wolten solche begabüng oder leibgedinge gnediglich schützen vnd handhaben

Aüch bitte ich alle meine güten freünde, wolten meiner lieben kethen zeügen sein vnd sie entschuldigen helffen, wo ettliche vnnütze meüler sie beschweren oder verünglimpfen wolten, als solt sie ettwa eine Barschafft hinder sich haben die sie den armen Kindern entwenden oder vnterschlagen würde. Ich bin des zeüge, das da keine Barschafft ist, on die Becher vnd kleinod, droben ym leibgedinge erzelet. Vnd zwar solts bey yderman die rechnung offentlich geben, weil man weis, Wie viel ich einkomens gehabt von M[einem] g[nädigsten] H[errn] herrn, vnd sonst nicht einen heller noch kornlin von yemand einzükomen gehabt, on was geschenk ist gewesen, welchs droben vnter den kleinoten. Züm teil aüch noch ynn der schuld steckt vnd zü finden ist

Vnd ich doch von solchem einkomen vnd geschenck so viel gebawet, gekaüff, grosse vnd schwere haüshaltüng gefürt Das ichs müs neben andern selbs für einen sonderlichen wünderlichen segen erkennen, das ichs habe konnen erschwingen, vnd nicht wunder ist das keine Barschafft, sondern das nicht mehr schüld da ist

Dis bitte ich darümb denn der Teüffel, so er mir nicht kündte neher komen, solt er wol meine kethe allein der vrsachen, allerley weise süchen, das sie des Mannes Doctor Martinüs eheliche haüsfraw gewest vnd (Gott lob) noch ist

Zü letzt bitte ich aüch ydermann, Weil ich ynn dieser begebüng oder leibgedinge, nicht braüche der jüristischen forme vnd worter (dazü ich vrsachen gehabt) Man wolle mich lassen sein die person, die ich doch ynn der warheit bin Nemlich offentlich, vnd die beide ym himel aüff erden, aüch ynn der Helle bekand, ansehens oder aütoritet gnüg hat der man trawen vnd gleüben mag mehr denn keinem Notario. Denn so mir verdampten, armen vnwirdigen elenden sünder, Gott der Vater aller Barmehertzickeit, das Eüangelion seines lieben Sons vertrawet, dazu mich aüch trew vnd warhafftig drinnen gemacht, bis her behalten vnd fünden hat, Also das aüch viel ynn der welt dasselb dürch mich angenomen, vnd mich für einen lerer der Warheit halten, vngeacht des Bapsts bann, Keisers, konige, fürsten, pfaffen, ia aller teüffel zorn Sol man ia viel mehr mir hie ynn dieser geringen sachen gleüben, sonderlich weil hie ist mein hand, fast wol bekand Der hoffnüng, Es solle gnüg sein wenn man sagen vnd beweisen kan, dis ist D Martinüs Luthers (der Gottes Notarius vnd zeüge ist ynn seinem Eüangelio) ernstliche vnd wolbedachte meinüng mit seiner eigen hand vnd siegel zü beweisen,

Geschehen vnd gegeben Am tage Epiphanie.

1 5 4 2

M Luther vts [ut supra]

Ego philippus Melanthon testor hanc esse et sententiam ac voluntatem et manum Reuerendi domini doctoris Martini Lutheri praeceptoris et patris nostri carissimi.

Et ego Caspar Creuciger d. testor hanc esse et sententiam et voluntatem et manum Reuerendi d. doctoris Martini Lutheri carissimi patris nostri. Quare et ipse mea manu subscripsi.

Et ego Johannes Bugenhagius Pomeranüs D. idem testor mea manü.

English translation

I Doctor Martin Luther declare in my own hand that I give to my dear and true wife, Katherin, for her maintenance (or whichever way you wish to put it) for life, to dispose over freely and for her own use. And I do so by the strength of this deed and on this day. Firstly

The small estate at Zülsdorf, as I bought it and improved it, with all things pertaining to it, as it has been in my possession

Secondly Haus Bruno as a dwelling, which I bought in Wolf's name[25]

Thirdly cups and jewellery, that is rings, chains and medals, both golden and silver, worth about a thousand guilders

I act thus

Firstly because, as a pious, loyal spouse she has always loved me, respected me and looked after me, giving birth to five living children (may God give them long life) thanks to God's rich bounty, raising them as well

Secondly so as to enable her to take on herself and pay all my debts (if I should not do so in my own lifetime), about 450 guilders to the best of my knowledge. Or perhaps it is even more than that

Thirdly and mostly because it is my wish that she should not be in the hands of the children but they in hers, respecting her, and being subjected to her, as God commanded. For I have truly seen and experienced how the devil makes use of evil and envious mouths, to bait and incite the children, though they be pious, especially if the mothers be widows, and the sons get wives and the daughters husbands, turning the mother-in-law against the daughter-in-law and the daughter-in-law against the mother-in-law

For I consider their own mother to be the best guardian of her own

Ich Martinus Luther Doctor etc beken-
ne mit dieser meiner eigen handschrifft
das ich meiner lieben und trewen hausfrawen
Katherin gegeben habe zum leibgedinge (oder
wie man das nennen kan) auff yhr lebelang,
damit sie yhres gefallens und zu yhrem besten
gebaren muge, Und gebe yhr das ym krafft
dieses brieues, gegenwertigs und heutiges tages

Nemlich, das gutlin Zulsdorff, wie ichs
selb gekaufft und zugericht habe, aller dinge
wie ichs bis daher gehabt habe,

Zum andern das Haus Brun zur wo-
nung, so ich unter meins Wolffs namen ge-
kaufft habe

Zum dritten, die Becher und Cleinot, als
ringe, Ketten, Gheschenck groschen, gulden und silbern
Welche ungeferlich solten bey tausent gulden
werd sein   Das thu ich darumb

Erstlich, das sie mich als ein from, trew
ehlich gemalh, allzeit, lieb, werd und schon ge-
halten, Und mir durch reichen Gottes segen
funff lebendige Kinder (die noch fur handen
Gott gebe lange) geboren und erzogen hat

Zum andern, das sie die schuld, so ich noch
schuldig bin (wo ich sie nicht bey leben ablege)
auff sich nemen und bezalen sol, Welcher mag
sein ungefer mir bewust, cccc l. fl. Mugen
sich villeicht wol mehr finden

Zum dritten und aller meist darumb, das ich wil
sie müsse nicht den kindern, sondern die kinder
sollen yhr ynn die hende sehen, sie ynn ehren
halten und unterworffen sein, wie Gott gebo
ten hat. Denn ich wol gesehen und erfaren, wie
der Teuffel, wider dis gebot, die kinder hetzet und
reitzet wenn sie gleich from sind, durch bose und
neidische Meuler sonderlich wenn die müttere
widwen sind, Und die Söne ehefrawen und
die töchtere ehemenner kriegen, und widerumb
Socrus Nurum Nurus Socrum. Denn
ich halt, das die Mutter werde yhrer eigen kinder
der beste fur münde sein, und solch gütlin und
leibgedinge nicht zu der kinder schaden oder
nachteil, sondern zu nütz und besserung
brauchen, als die yhr fleisch und blut sind
und sie unter yhrem hertzen getragen hat
Und ob sie nach meinem tode genottigt
oder sonst verursacht würde (denn ich Gott
ynn seinen wercken und willen kein zil setzen
kan) sich zu verendern, so traue ich doch und
wil hiemit solchs vertrawet haben, sie werde
sich mütterlich gegen unser beider kinder halten
Und alles trewlich, es sey leibgedinge oder an
ders, wie recht ist, mit yhnen teilen
Und bitte auch hie mit unterthenigklich
meinen gnedigsten herrn Hertzog Johans Friderichen
Kurfürsten zu S. etc. wolten solche begabung
oder leibgedinge gnediglich schützen und handhaben

Auch bitte ich alle meine guten freunde, wol-
ten meiner lieben Kethen zeugen sein und sie
entschuldigen helffen, wo etliche unnutze meuler
sie beschweren oder verunglimpffen wolten, als
solt sie etwa eine barschafft hinder sich haben
die sie den armen kindern entwenden oder
unterschlahen würde. Ich bin des zeuge, das
da keine barschafft ist, on die becher und
kleinod, droben ym leibgeding erzelet. Und
zwar solts bey yderman die rechnung offentlich
geben, weil man weis, wie viel ich ein-
komens gehabt von M. g. H. herrn. Und
sonst nicht einen heller noch kornlein von
yemand einzukomen gehabt, on was geschenck
ist gewesen, welchs droben unter den klei-
noten, zum teil auch noch ym der schuld
steckt und zu finden ist. Und ich doch
von solchem einkomen und geschenck, so viel
gebawet, gekaufft, grosse und schwere haushal-
tung gefurt, das ichs, mus neben andern selbs
fur einen sonderlichen wunderlichen segen er-
kennen, das ichs habe konnen erschwingen, und
nicht wunder ist, das keine barschafft, sondern
das nicht mehr schulds da ist. Das
bitte ich darumb. Denn der Teuffel, so er mir nicht
kunde neher komen, solt er wol meine Kethe
allein der ursachen, allerley weise suchen, das
sie des Mannes, Doctor Martinus eheliche
haussfraw gewest und (Gott lob) noch ist

Zu letzt bitte ich auch yderman Weil ich ynn
dieser begabung oder leibgedinge, nicht brauche
der Juristischen formen vnd wortter (dazu ich
vrsachen gehabt) Man wolle mich lassen sein
die person, die ich doch ynn der warheit bin
Nemlich, offentlich, vnd die beide ynn himel
auff erden, auch ynn der helle bekand, an=
sehens oder autoritet gnug hat, der man trawen
vnd gleuben mag mehr denn keinem Notario
Denn so mir verdampten, armen, vnwirdigen
elenden sunder, Gott der Vater aller barmher=
tzikeit, das Euangelion seines lieben sons vertrawet, dazu mich auch trew vnd warhafftig
darynnen gemacht, bis her behalten vnd funden
hat, Also das auch viel ynn der welt dasselb
durch mich angenomen, Vnd mich fur einen
lerer der Warheit halten, vngeacht des Bapsts
bann, keisers, koniges, fursten, pfaffen, ia aller
teuffel zorn, Sol man ia viel mehr mir hie
ynn dieser geringen sachen gleuben, Sonderlich
weil hie ist meine hand, fast wol bekand, Der
hoffnung es solle gnug sein Wenn man sagen
vnd beweisen kan, dis ist D Martinus Luthers
(der Gottes Notarius vnd zeuge ist ynn seinem
Euangelio) ernstliche vnd wolbedachte meinung
mit seiner eigen hand vnd siegel zu beweisen,

Geschrieben vnd gegeben Am tage Epiphanie
1542

M Luther

Ego Philippus Melanthon testor hanc esse
sententiam ac voluntatem et manum
Reverendi dni doctoris Martini Lutheri
praeceptoris et patris nostri carissimi.

Et ego Caspar Cruciger d. testor hanc esse
et sententiam et voluntatem et manum
Reverendi d. doctoris Martinj Lutheri
carissimi patris nostri. Quare et ipse
mea manu subscripsi.

Et ego Johannes Bugenhagius Pomeranus d. idem testor manu mea.

[illegible]

children, using goods and chattels not to the hurt and disadvantage but to the advantage and improvement of the children who are her flesh and blood and she carried them under her heart.

And even if after my death she should feel forced or otherwise caused (for I cannot set an aim for God in His works or will) to alter her state, I still trust and have placed my confidence in that she will be a mother to the children of us both, and truly share chattels and other things with them, as is only right

And hereby I also most humbly ask my gracious lord, His Electoral Grace, Duke John Frederick, Elector etc., to protect and implement this gift and maintenance graciously

I also ask all my good friends to bear witness for my dear Kate, and help protect her, should useless mouths accuse and slander her, for instance that she had ready money hidden away somewhere which she meant to extract from her poor children, embezzling it. I bear witness that there is no ready money, except the cups and jewels listed above amongst the goods. The accounts should be clear to everyone since it is known what income I had of my gracious lord, and not a penny or grain from anyone else, except for the gifts which are above, amongst the jewels. Some of it are pledged for debts and to be found there

That from this income and those gifts I was able to build and buy much and to pay the expenses of a large and difficult household, that I managed to do so, I and others must reckon a special and miraculous bounty, and let them not wonder that there is no ready money, but that the debts are not greater

I ask for that since the devil, unable to get any closer to me, will surely try and do so with my Kate by all means, if for no other reason than that she was and (God be praised) still is, the lawful wife of her husband Doctor Martin

Finally I ask everyone, not having used legal forms and terms in this deed of gift or maintenance (for which I had good reason), to recognise me for the man I am in truth and publicly, as one who carries sufficient respect and authority in heaven and on earth, and in hell as well, to be trusted and believed more than any notary. For if God the father of all mercy has entrusted the Gospel of His own dear Son to me, a damned, poor, unworthy sinner, making me loyal and true in that service, and preserving and finding me that up to now, so that many in the world have taken it up through me, holding me to be a teacher of the truth, in spite of the papal interdict and the anger of the Emperor, of kings, princes and priests and of all the devils. I should then be believed all the more in this small matter, especially since this is my own hand which is well known. I hope it is enough to be able to say and prove that this is the serious and well-considered will of D. Martin Luther (who is God's notary and witness to His Gospel) proved with his own hand and seal,

Made and delivered on the day of the Epiphany.

1 5 4 2

M. Luther

I Philipp Melanthon [sic] bear witness that this is the decree, will and hand of the Reverend Martin Luther, our dear teacher and father.

And I d. Caspar Creuciger bear witness that this is the decree, will and hand of the Reverend Doctor Martin Luther, our dear father. That is why I too sign in my own hand.

And I Doctor Johannes Bugenhagen of Pomerania also bear witness to the same with my own hand.

This well-considered second will contains, in comparison with the first produced in a fever, less sharp comment directed at the papacy and more tender concern for the family. Two years later, on 1 February 1544, in court proceedings conducted by Hans Lufft (the Wittenberg town magistrate and renowned printer) "as an advocate, and on the orders of the honourable and learned man Martin Luther, Doctor of Holy Writ", significant clauses were added to the testament prior to its being recorded by the Court.[26] By these provisions Katharina Luther was given the Haus Bruno not only as a dwelling but for her use at will. In addition those pieces of real estate in Wittenberg which were to be transferred from Luther to his wife were listed—three gardens and a field—naming the former owners and giving their precise location. This list, the sole regular appendage to what was otherwise a highly irregular document, is now in the Town Archives at Wittenberg.

On 20 February 1544, when the Elector heard of Luther's death, he wrote to Katharina undertaking care of the family. The following day he sent one hundred guilders to the university to clear a debt she had incurred. At her request, he appointed guardians of her choosing for the children: Luther's brother Jakob, the court physician Dr Matthias Ratzeberger, and Ambrosius Reuter, the burgomaster of the day, with Melanchthon and Cruciger as substitutes. In addition he agreed to pay a pension of two thousand guilders a year to the children, five hundred guilders for each child.

On 11 April Elector John Frederick confirmed the will and declared it legally valid. Within the year he helped Katharina to purchase Wachsdorf near Wittenberg, a knightly estate formerly owned by Dr Sebald Münster, a friend of Luther's who had died young. The counts of Mansfeld also contributed two thousand guilders to the purchase price.

Luther's will may have been odd from a legal point of view but it did succeed in providing for his family up to their death. Haus Bruno and the Zülsdorf estate were sold after Katharina Luther died. A copper engraving of the first survives, and a memorial stone erected in 1817, with the inscription "Martin Luther lived here", marks the place of the second. Nothing is known of the fate of most of the gold and silverware, cups etc. A silver-gilt cup, the wedding present of the University of Wittenberg, is in Greifswald, the two wedding rings are in Brunswick, and a glass given by Gustavus Vasa of Sweden is in Leipzig.

A Hungarian Attends an Auction

After probate was granted the will disappeared for a century and a half. A publicly accessible copy existed (and still exists) in the Town Archives of Weimar, with an authenticating note in Melanchthon's hand. A complete text was included in the Altenburg edition of Luther's works. The first hint of its whereabouts was given in 1706 by the German historian Christian Juncker in his *Das guldene und silberne Ehrengedächtnis D. Martini Lutheri* (The Gold and Silver Memorial of Dr Martin Luther) which summarised the scholarly debate:

> *Seckendorff's Lib. III Fol. 651, as well as D. Johann Friedrich Mayer's* Schediasmata de vita Catharina a Bora *both discuss Luther's will. The text itself is printed in Part 8 of Luther's writings, Altenburg edition, Fol. 846, which states that the will was dated on Euphemia's Day [i.e. 16 September]. The reverend Dr Samuel Benedict Carpzovius, Senior Church Counsellor of the Electorate of Saxony and Senior Court Preacher at Dresden, has, however, kindly informed me that he not only possesses the true original of the said will, which was signed by Melanchthon, Cruciger, and Bugenhagen, but that the latter shows it to be dated on the day of the Epiphany and not Euphemia's Day, not to mention minor differences between the original and the printed copy in a number of details.*

The family of Samuel Benedict Carpzow were long established as Lutheran scholars in Saxony. Professor Johann Benedict Carpzow, great-grandnephew of Samuel Benedict and the last male to bear the family name, was born in 1720 and died in 1803. His large collection of books and manuscripts was auctioned the following spring, the catalogue being compiled by his son-in-law Henke. The third item on page nine of the catalogue was Luther's holograph of the 1542 will and a letter (presumed to be authentic) written in 1533 and addressed to Philipp of Hessen, both in a red velvet case.

The case and its contents were bought by a well-known Hungarian collector, Miklós Jankovich, a Catholic born in Pest in 1772. The verso of the will bears a Latin note in an unidentified hand stating that he (Jankovich) paid forty ducats for the will at the Helmstedt auction of Carpzow's library. Jankovich was a generous benefactor of the Hungarian National Library, and his acquisition of the Luther will and of several letters by Luther and Melanchthon was welcomed by many of his contemporaries, including the poet Ferenc Kazinczy (who refers to it in a letter of 1808) and István Horváth who noted in his diary: "Visited the Honourable Miklós Jankovich and again saw the original of Martin Luther's will which this indefatigable searcher and finder of antiquities brought home for us from Germany." Horváth was the first director of the Hungarian National Library.

It is clear from a letter to the General Consistory of Pest, dated 15 February 1815, that Jankovich donated the will along with some eighty other documents from the Reformation period, to the Hungarian Lutheran Church. Indeed, he confirmed this earlier letter in a second (in Latin) on 10 November 1832. But as the Church possessed no proper archives at the time, the collection remained temporarily in the custody of the donor. Doubtless, his expensive enthusiasm for manuscripts contributed to the financial troubles Jankovich soon found himself in, and he was forced to seek a buyer for his personal collection. Finally, the Hungarian National Library agreed to buy part of it; by the contract signed in the autumn of 1831 the objects purchased were to remain in Jankovich's custody until the completion of a new museum building which was to include the National Library. The third clause of the contract stated that Luther's will, donated to the Hungarian Lutheran congregation in Pest, was not included. The Calvinist Church of Hungary and the Roman Catholic parish of Rácalmás also received a number of devotional items.

The minutes of the Hungarian Lutheran Church frequently refer to the Jankovich donation and in particular to the Luther will. In 1838, Baron Sándor Prónay, lay head of the Church, petitioned the Archduke Joseph to transfer the document from the museum to the General Consistory. An answer the following year explained the difficulty of transfer by referring to the great floods of 1838 and the need to take the document from the safe repository found for it then first to the new museum building. Years passed before the Church came into actual possession of the document. Some extracts from the minutes of the General Consistory chart the frustration of the

Church, and these are all the more interesting in that Lajos Kossuth, leader of the 1848–49 revolution in Hungary and the War of Independence against the Habsburgs, was among the members:

1840: *protocol 10 "The clerk to the Consistory reports that Martin Luther's will donated by Miklós Jankovich could not be extracted yet from the papers of the National Museum. The President is entrusted to obtain it as soon as possible and present it to the Consistory."*
1841: *protocol 8 "That as soon as the building of the National Museum is completed the President solicit the handing over of Martin Luther's will."*
1842: *protocol 12 "...that it be extracted from the Museum building in good time."*
1843: *protocol 12 "The Clerk reports that Martin Luther's will can be obtained from the National Museum, the Honourable President is therefore asked to fetch it, and place it in the General Archives."*
1844: *protocol 13 "The Honourable President is requested to fetch Martin Luther's original will, and place it in the General Archives."*
And finally,
1845: *protocol S. 17 "A letter from Ágoston Kubinyi, Director of the Museum, addressed to the General Consistory, was presented... showing that [he] was sending the original document by Royal Court Councillor Lajos Schedius the Elder so that it could be placed in the General Archives of the General Consistory, which he has already done, since, as Councillor Schedius has just reported, the document is already in the General Archives."*

In this way, Luther's will finally arrived in the possession of its legal owners, in the custody of Lajos Schedius, archivist to the Church. Not that there were not dissenting voices: the 1845 minutes record a view that "it would be to our greater honour securing greater publicity for this glorious object, if it were left in the National Museum." The 1846 minutes show that a resolution of this difference of opinion was postponed while lithograph copies for display in all dioceses were prepared. Kubinyi, director of the National Museum and a member of the Consistory, was put in charge of the operation: one of the copies was sent promptly to Eisleben, Luther's birthplace, at the suggestion of Lajos Schedius. Finally, the Consistory resolved to retain the document in its red velvet case. It was placed inside a steel case, within the added security of a safe, and remained there until once again it found itself at the centre of controversy.

Disputes over Authenticity

During the War of Independence of 1848–49 in Hungary, and the Austrian oppression which followed, Luther's will in Budapest received little attention either at home or abroad. Only the *Protestantische Jahrbücher* discussed it, in an article which was probably the source of reports in the *Dresdner Constitutionelle Zeitung* in 1859, and the *Zeitschrift für historische Theologie* in 1860. Carl August Hugo Burckhardt in *Dr Martin Luthers Briefwechsel* (Martin Luther's Correspondence), published in 1866, explicitly stated his belief that the original of the will was in the general archives of the Lutheran Church of Hungary.

In 1878 a meeting of the General Consistory appointed a six-man committee to examine the genuineness of all the documents in its archives. On 13 November the six experts visited the archives, and presented their report the following year. In view of the counterclaims which were subsequently made, the credentials of the committee should be recorded: they were Baron Albert Nyáry, historian and expert on heraldry; Ferenc Pulszky, formerly a diplomat on Kossuth's staff, art historian and director of the National Museum; Mihály Zsilinszky, an historian and later undersecretary of state; and, representing the clergy, Sándor Doleschall, the German Lutheran pastor in Pest; Vilmos Győry, poet, translator, and the Hungarian Lutheran pastor in Pest, and Lajos Haan, historian, member of the Academy, and archdeacon of Békéscsaba.

Some extracts from the committee's report will establish the quality of their research:

> *In the case of Luther's 1542 will we examined the paper of the document in the first place and found that it had a double watermark—one consisting of the Saxon coat of arms and the electoral hat, the other of an F*

and an eagle—and found that it was really from the country and time in which Luther lived.[28]

Concerning the appearance of the holograph, the following ought to be added. The document, on small foolscap, covers five and half pages, and contains one hundred and twenty-six lines, including the signature of the witnesses. It is in a splendid state of preservation. It was originally folded, as a brown line on the paper indicates, in the manner of letters, or small documents, such as I.O.U.s, which are folded at both ends towards the middle. – At present it is in its natural size in the red silk, or rather red velvet cover described by Henke. – The seal referred to in the closing words must have been below the date, next to the testator's signature, as a brownish stain indicates. – The sixth side of the manuscript, which served as cover, legibly bears the yellowed words: "Catharin Lutherin Leipgeding".[29]

We compared the manuscript itself with
a) a letter written by Luther on Saint Donatus' Day, 1535, to the Elector John, at present in the Archives of the Hungarian National Museum [the letter was destroyed during the Second World War].
b) the facsimile of Luther's handwriting dated 1542, at present in the possession of Archdeacon Lajos Haan,
c) a Luther holograph of his younger years, Von der Freiheit eines Christenmenschen *(Of the Freedom of a Christian Man), which found its way to Bishop Michael Schwarz of Eperjes via Johann Christian Kress, Johann Sigmund Mörl of Nuremberg and Samuel Bredeczky, moderator of Galicia. Schwarz donated it to the General Archives...*[30]

Having thus established the authenticity of Luther's will the committee recommended that it should be taken from the general collection of documents of lesser value and placed on public display. Their report, which was published in *Pesti Hírlap* in 1879 and two years later in German in the *Ungarische Revue,* aroused considerable interest both in Hungary and abroad.

Shortly after the publication of the report in *Pesti Hírlap* an article appeared in the popular *Wiener Fremdenblatt.* In it a certain Karl Reuss, describing himself as a "historian by profession", maintained that the committee had not been made up of experts but of "celebrated parliamentary orators". He went on to provide an alternative account of the provenance of Luther's original will:

Ranke in his History of the Reformation, which was based on thorough research, had conclusively shown after all that Luther's only holograph will was at present in the Heidelberg Library, where it is still exhibited under glass and in a frame; that Luther's allegedly original will... in Hungary is not by him, but by his disciple Honterus, a Saxon from Kronstadt, who had introduced the Reformation to Transylvania, one of Luther's friends. When Honterus travelled to Germany in 1549, three years after Luther's death, to see his great friend and teacher's tomb, Luther's widow permitted the making of several copies of the original will which was still in her possession, in gratitude for the presents of the Transylvanian Saxons...[31]

All this was presented with such a display of authority that even experts in Hungary began to doubt their own conclusions. E. A. Doleschall appealed to Karl Reuss through a number of Austrian papers to provide evidence for his claims, at the very least to give a precise reference to the point where Ranke allegedly discussed Honterus' copying of Luther's will. Though nothing was heard from Reuss, his theory was being more widely circulated in the press. Impressed by the citation of Ranke as an authority, the balance of opinion swung towards the Reuss theory, so that a literary supplement to a Lutheran journal declared confidently in 1879 that "the conclusion must be drawn that Luther's sole holograph will is at present in the Heidelberg Library, where it is still exhibited and under glass."[32]

Two significant dissenters from this consensus emerged. The first was Zangemeister, the librarian at Heidelberg who wrote to Doleschall in answer to an inquiry specifically denying that any such document was on display.[33] Even more damaging to Reuss was a letter from Leopold von Ranke himself to Doleschall confessing "that I cannot recall ever having expressed an opinion on Luther's will in any of my writings" and adding that a friend had checked all possible sources for any forgotten allusion.[34] Who then was this "historian by profession" who had launched the Heidelberg theory? Neither the *Wiener Fremdenblatt,* which had sponsored it, nor any other paper could provide Doleschall with any information on Karl Reuss and his name fails to appear in any work of reference. It must be concluded that the name was a pseudonym and that what was at stake was not Luther's will but some professional jealousy or intrigue. This was not the last such intrigue to implicate Luther's will.

Secret Manœuvres

For many years the will lay in almost total obscurity. On rare occasions, such as the fourth centenary of the Reformation, it was written up by church historians, but for the most part it drew little or no attention to itself. Then, a few years before the outbreak of the Second World War, controversy began to rumble once again. Those involved were a dozen Nazi politicians and diplomats from the German Third Reich and an Austrian and a German expert. This concluding chapter to the stormy history of the document has been made possible only by the kindness of those in charge of Lutherhalle in Wittenberg who have made the relevant documents available to the present writer.

Essentially, the twentieth-century intrigue concerning Luther's will revolves round the activities of Hermann von Trenkwald, an art "adviser" and museum curator in Vienna. On 26 August 1936 he launched a campaign to repatriate Luther's will to Germany and Wittenberg—repatriate it, that is, to the Nazi Reich. His opening move was to establish communications with Oskar Thulin, director of the Lutherhalle in Wittenberg to whom he mentioned Doleschall's account of the nineteenth-century controversy between Heidelberg and Budapest. Through his access to the German embassy in Budapest, and his acquaintance with Franz von Papen who was German ambassador in Vienna, Trenkwald thought his objective was entirely practicable. His attitude may be gauged from the letter to Thulin, "Given the current political situation... this business might prove more easy to transact than one might imagine. Let us exploit this circumstance and make a direct approach to the objective!"

Thulin did in fact open negotiations with the Hungarian Lutherans, Dezső Kuthy their Secretary-General, and Baron Albert Radvánszky the Inspector General, though his motives as head of the Lutherhalle were in themselves perhaps unexceptionable. Trenkwald, on the other hand, only involved the Hungarians in preliminary negotiations, and did not share Thulin's reservations about compensation and so forth. Over a period of five months Trenkwald attempted to arrange a personal meeting with the head of the Lutherhalle who by this time was no longer answering his letters. Following the *Anschluss* of 1938, and Germany's further advance on the Danube, Trenkwald decided that he might be able to involve a far more prestigious patron than Thulin in his campaign to repatriate the great reformer's will.

Before the outbreak of war he attempted to use one Schulte-Straathaus, an emissary travelling on Reich Chancellery business, as an intermediary between Wittenberg, Budapest, Hitler's office and himself. Professor Thulin of Wittenberg, however, had been visiting Hungary at this time in connection with a projected statue of Luther to be erected in Budapest, and he appreciated the resistance of the Hungarian Lutherans to any such plan. The outbreak of war postponed further consultations, and eighteen months passed before Trenkwald persuaded Thulin to meet Roth, a senior Foreign Ministry official, on 28 October 1940. Roth agreed to speak to Martin Bormann in Hitler's headquarters, and in fact did so. On 29 October, Trenkwald wrote to Thulin requesting a revaluation of the will at one hundred thousand Reichmarks, ten times the sum contemplated by Thulin three years earlier:

> *Both of us* [i.e. Trenkwald and Thulin] *ought to sign the draft. Bormann would thus hold something in writing when going in to see the Führer. I still have a copy of my extracts from Doleschall's history of Luther's will which I shall attach. All other aspects* [negotiations initiated by the Foreign Ministry] *will be verbally communicated to Bormann. I should not be surprised if Bormann suggests that we present our case to the Führer personally. The Führer knows me, and personally addressed me and my wife when we met two years ago in the Künstlerhaus in Munich.*

Thulin completed his draft on 4 November, and he and Trenkwald took it to Bormann. The following day Trenkwald wrote once again to Thulin on the subject of the ten per cent (or more) he expected as commission on the negotiation.

In this way Martin Luther's will became a subject of discussion at Hitler's headquarters in the autumn of 1940. It seemed at first as if these discussions must reach a positive conclusion quickly, and

Bormann told Trenkwald that the purchase of the will by Hitler would be arranged directly by Hans Heinrich Lammers, head of the Reich Chancellery. But the prospects of an early conclusion were dulled somewhat by the German Cultural Attaché in Budapest who advised a postponement of negotiations with the Hungarian Church until February 1941. On 21 January, Professor Thulin forwarded to Dr du Mesnil, a senior government official, a copy of a draft prepared three years earlier in which he stressed both the devotion of Hungarian Lutherans to the memory of their founder and the need to respect the independence of the Hungarian congregations.

Meanwhile relations between Trenkwald the dealer, and Thulin the curator at Wittenberg, continued to deteriorate. Trenkwald accused Thulin of conducting private negotiations, and Thulin was invited to call on officials in the Chancellery to discuss his position. On 7 March Thulin wrote to Roth in the Foreign Ministry to the effect that he did not wish to include Trenkwald in negotiations with the Lutheran Church in Budapest. By 11 June, Roth was rebuking Thulin for suggestions that Trenkwald might seek some financial compensation for himself—"Have you any reason to believe that he expects such compensation, or that he is financially interested in the business?"

Thulin undoubtedly wished to see the will on display in the Lutherhalle at Wittenberg where forty thousand visitors might see it each year. In place of purchase, with all the dubious interests which might attach themselves to the transaction, he suggested that the document be placed on permanent loan by the Hungarian Church, the ceremonial handing over to take place in the Führer's presence. According to a letter from Roth to Thulin on 21 May, Trenkwald's contribution to this new discussion was the suggestion that the German Reich should offer the Hungarians in exchange for the Luther will a fifteenth-century breviary of György Pálóczi, archbishop of Esztergom, from the Salzburg State Library.

By late May it was clear that Kuthy, Secretary-General of the Hungarian Church, had indicated the unlikelihood of Luther's will being transferred to Germany. Finally, on 26 June, Baron Albert Radvánszky and Béla Kapi (the senior bishop) informed Oskar Thulin that his request had been examined but that the terms of the Jankovich donation did not permit the transfer of Luther's will. Though it was suggested that the question might be reconsidered in quieter times, this letter on behalf of the Presidium of the Lutheran Church of Hungary effectively ended negotiations open and secret.

Epilogue

In this essay I have tried to trace the background of Martin Luther's will, the story of its composition, and its subsequent career. What lends particular weight and value to this four hundred and forty year-old document is the character of its author. This is the last will and testament of a man who changed the features of European Christianity within three decades and to whom nations owe the enfranchisement of their own native languages.

One of the consequences of the medieval church's teaching on justification by good works was that many left their property to the church. Luther fought against such a view. The recognition of gratuitous grace and justification by faith alone allowed him to see and proclaim that God had liberated man to serve his fellow men and attend to their needs with loving care. Luther therefore had no wish in his will to give gifts to God to reconcile him—he knew that such action could not lay up treasures in heaven—but wished instead to make provision for those in his care, his family, showing love that bore in mind every possibility and aspect of the future.

Luther reinterpreted piety, reinterpreted attitudes towards the family, marriage, and family morality. A more modern view of life suffuses his will just as his teaching as a whole does. What lies behind this change is not simply the casting aside of monastic habit for a layman's clothes and a happy marriage but the recognition which allowed him to reinterpret the dogmas of centuries. By liberating the human conscience he also increased human responsibility.

His will reflects his views as a reformer on marriage, married life, and the family. As against the medieval church he thought of marriage and even sex as linked to creation, and not redemption. He thought marriage itself as of this world, as a secular business. Its aim was to create a community of body and soul for life and to continue the human race. He thought of priestly celibacy as running counter to

God's will. In his view it was this close communion of body and soul which protected the marriage partners at times of conflict, disappointment, or illness. By being ahead of his time, making a will in favour of his wife, he gave an example and pointed the way towards the equality of the sexes. That is how the great reformer, "God's notary", gave back to his contemporaries their good conscience, genuine humanity and mutual respect.

Notes

References to Luther's works are to the *Weimarer Ausgabe* (WA); TR stands for *Tischreden* (Table Talk), and Br for *Briefe* (Letters).

1 WA, TR vol 5, p. 168.
2 WA, Br. vol 11, p. 304.
3 WA, Br. vol 10, p. 305.
4 See Heinrich Bornkamm's postscript to Boehmer's *Der junge Luther* (Leipzig, 1951 4th ed. p. 358) concerning Luther's mother's maiden name.
5 WA, Br. vol 3, p. 394.
6 WA, TR vol 4, p. 503.
7 WA, Br. vol 3, p. 533.
8 WA, Br. vol 3, p. 522.
9 WA, Br. vol 3, p. 531.
10 Cited by Julius Köstlin and Gustav Kawerau *Martin Luther, sein Leben und seine Schriften*. Berlin, 1903 vol 2, p. 391.
11 *Ibid.* vol 2, p. 489.
12 WA, TR vol 4, p. 504.
13 WA, Br. vol 7, pp. 316–317.
14 Cited by K. E. Förstemann *D. Martin Luthers Testamente aus den Jahren 1537 und 1542*. Nordhausen, 1846. p. 16.
15 WA, TR vol 3, p. 90.
16 See Johann Friedrich Mayer *Ehrengedächtnis der Katherina Lutherin*. Frankfurt, Leipzig, 1724. p. 99.
17 WA, Br. vol 9, pp. 174, 205, and 267.
18 WA, Br. vol 11, p. 149.
19 WA, Br. vol 9, pp. 576–578.
20 WA, Br. vol 8, pp. 49–50.
21 WA, Br. vol 8, p. 51.
22 WA, Br. vol 8, pp. 55–56.
23 WA, TR vol 4, no. 5041.
24 WA, Br. vol 9, p. 123.
25 I.e. Wolf Sieberger, one of Luther s disciples.
26 WA, Br. vol 9, p. 575.
27 C. A. H. Burckhardt *Dr. Martin Luthers Briefwechsel*. Leipzig, 1866. p. 405.

28 E. A. Doleschall *Luthers Testament. Mit einer Photolithographie der Originalurkunde.* Budapest, Vienna, Leipzig, 1881. p. 1.
29 *Ibid.* p. 13.
30 *Ibid.* p. 2.
31 Cited by Doleschall *op. cit.* p. 4.
32 See *Allgemeine Evang. Luth. Kirchenzeitung,* vol 11, no 44, 1879.
33 Doleschall p. 7.
34 See Doleschall p. 6.

1 *Eisleben. The house in which Luther was born*

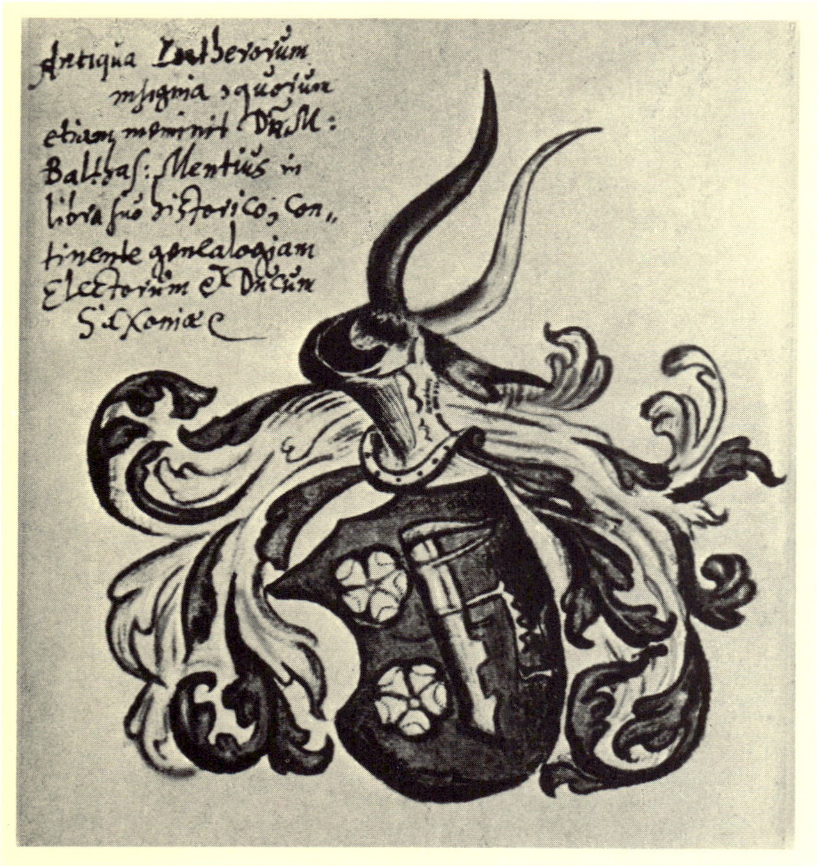

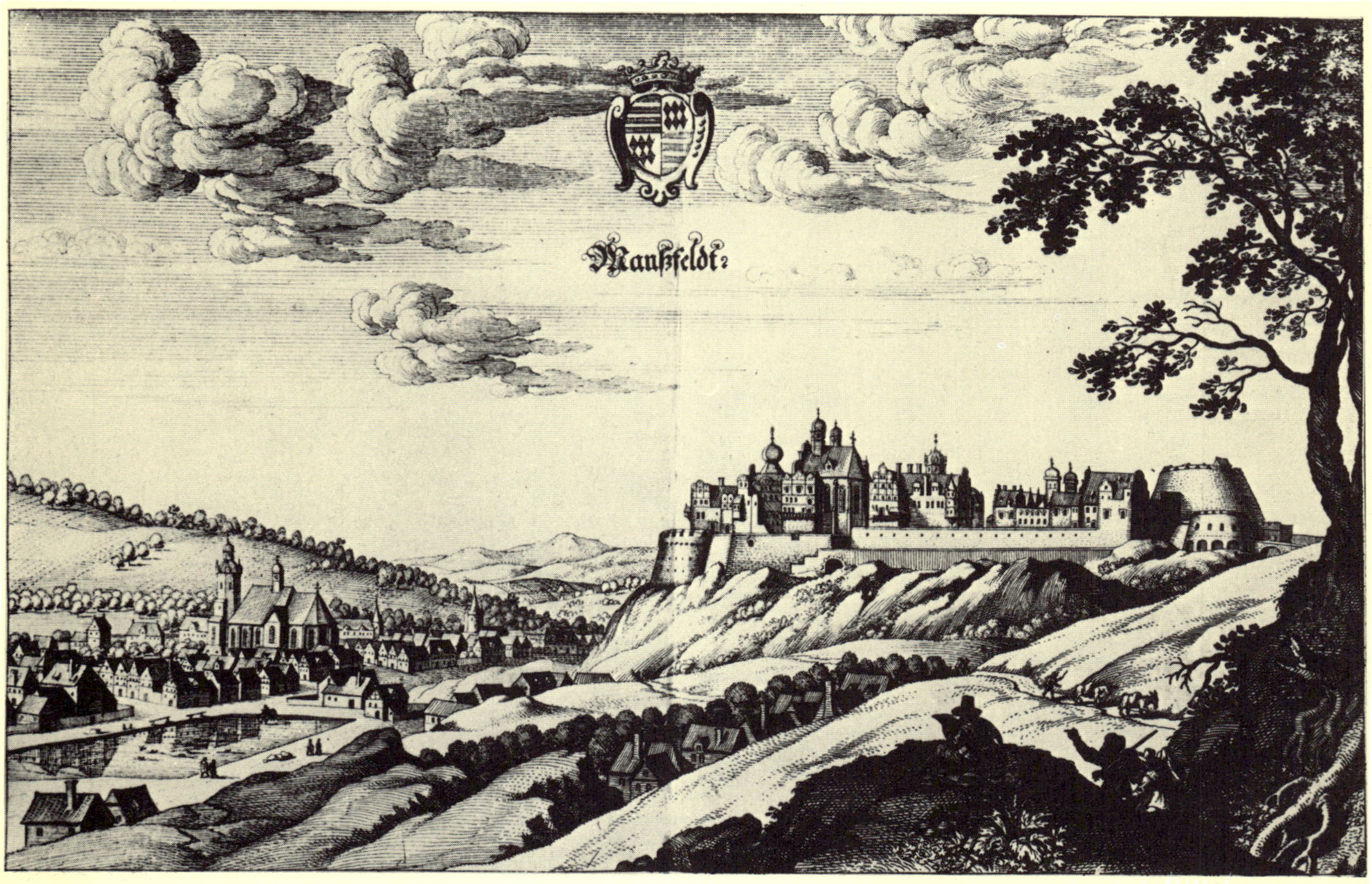

2 *The coat of arms of the Luther family*
3 *The castle and town of Mansfeld (copper engraving by Merian, c. 1650)*

4 *The town seal of Wittenberg (mid-16th century)*
5 *Wittenberg (woodcut by H. M. Deutsch, 1550)*

6 *Two nuns (copper engraving by F. Brun, late 16th century)*
7 *Two monks (copper engraving by F. Brun, late 16th century)*

8 *The monk Martin Luther (copper engraving by Lucas Cranach the Elder, 1520)*

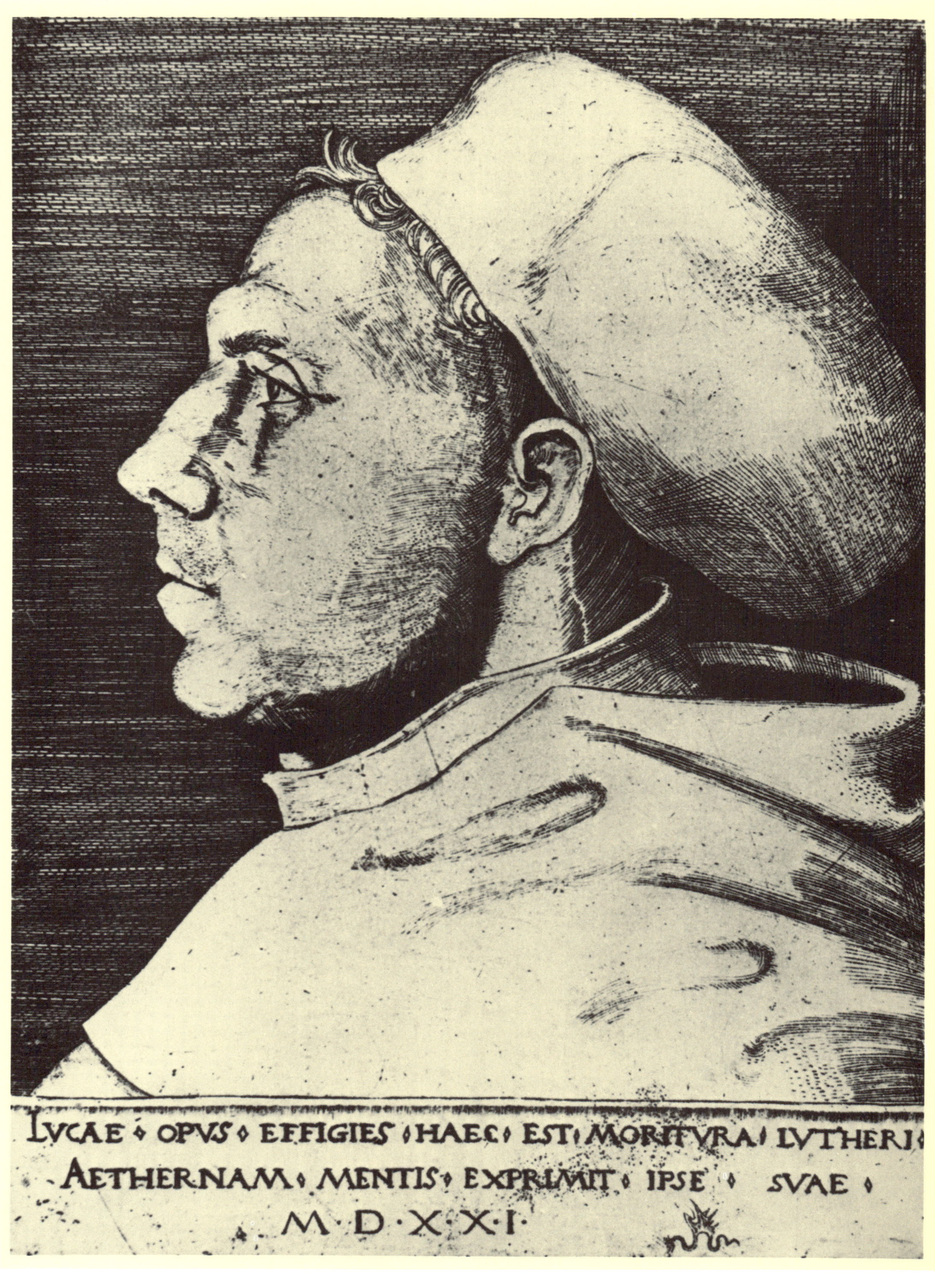

9 *Martin Luther (copper engraving by Lucas Cranach the Elder, 1521)*

10 *Katharina von Bora, Luther's wife (Lucas Cranach the Elder, 1525)*

11 *The Lutherhaus in Wittenberg (copper engraving by G. A. Lehmann, c. 1800)*

12 *The northern wing of the Wittenberg Lutherhaus, the Lutherhalle*

13 The Katharinenportal of the Wittenberg Lutherhaus

14 Reliefs of the Katharinenportal: Luther and the Luther rose (1540)

15 *Market-place and town church in Wittenberg*
16 *John Frederick the Magnificent, Elector of Saxony (copper engraving by G. Pencz, 1543)*
17 *Martin Luther (oil painting by Lucas Cranach the Elder, c. 1540)*

18 *Luther's fight for the true faith (an allegory by H. S. Beham, woodcut, early 16th century)*

19 *The seven-headed Luther (a contemporary woodcut caricatur attributed to H. Brosamer)*

20 *Martin Luther (oil painting by Lucas Cranach the Younger, 1543)*

21 *Luther as Saint Jerome (copper engraving by W. Stuber, late 16th century)*

22 *Philipp Melanchthon (after a copper engraving by Albrecht Dürer)*

23 *Luther and the other reformers shown as Christ's disciples at the Last Supper (altarpiece in oils in the Dessau-Mildensee church by Lucas Cranach the Younger, 1565)*

24 The house in which Luther died at Eisleben
25 The room in which Luther died

26 *Luther's death mask (Lutherhalle, Wittenberg)*

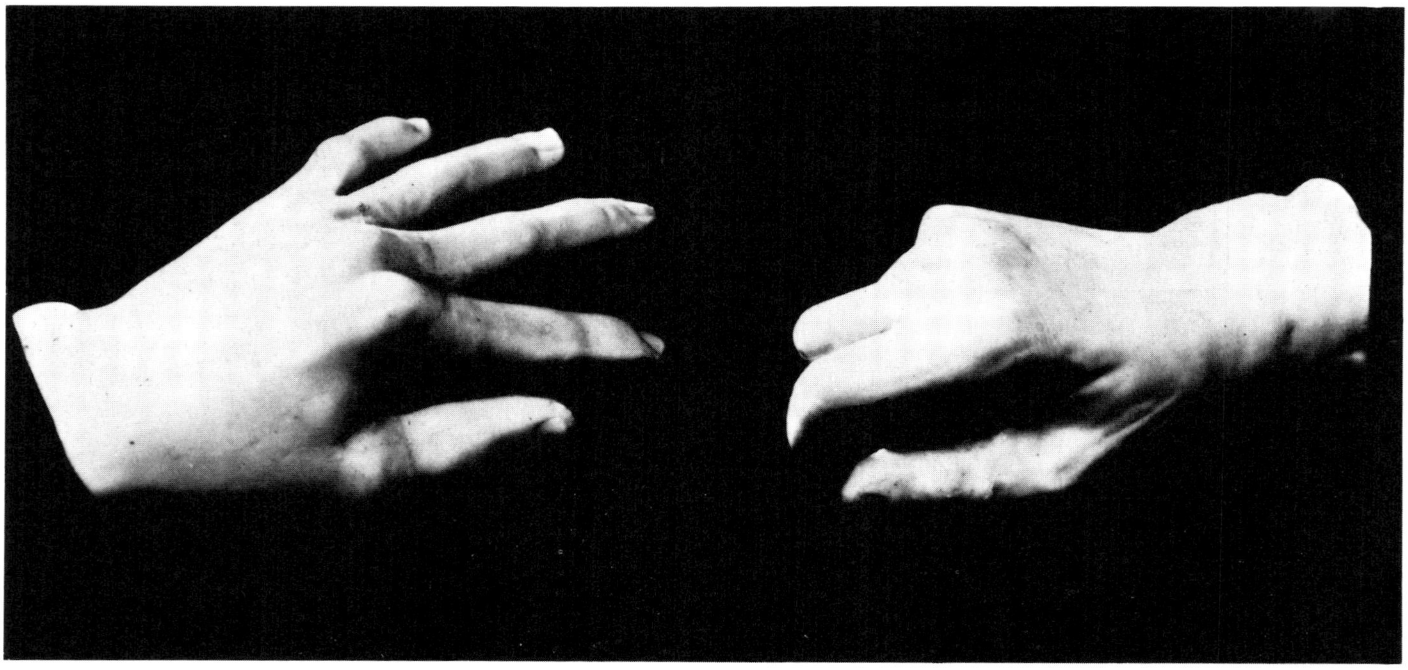

27 *Wax impression of Luther's hands after death (Lutherhalle, Wittenberg)*

28 *The Wittenberg Castle Church from the southeast*

HANC
D·MARTINI LVTHERI
TABVLAM·SEPVLCRALEM AD INSTAR
ARCHETYPI ACCVRATISSIME EXPRESSAM
ABBAS ET CONVENTVS COENOBII LVCCENSIS
PIETATIS CAVSA DEDICAVERVNT·

MARTINI LVTERI· S· THEOLO·
GIÆ·D·CORPVS·H·L·S·E·QVI·
AN·CHRISTI·M·D·XLVI·XII·
CAL·MARTII·EYSLEBII·IN·PA·
TRIA·S·M·O·C·V·ANN·LXIII·
·M·II·D·X·

29 Luther's tomb in the Wittenberg Castle Church
30 Cover-slab of Luther's tomb
31 Miklós Jankovich who took the will to Hungary

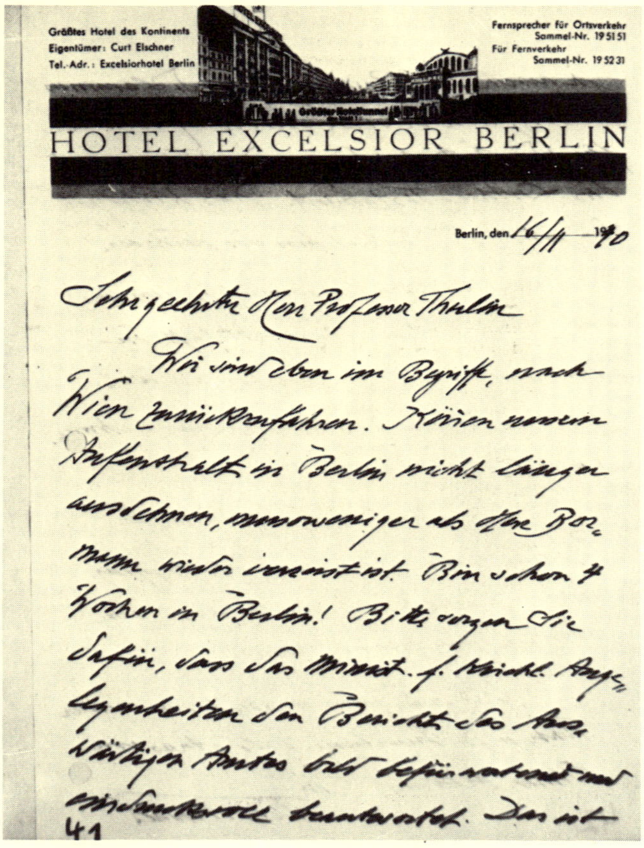
Größtes Hotel des Kontinents
Eigentümer: Curt Elschner
Tel. Adr.: Excelsiorhotel Berlin

Fernsprecher für Ortsverkehr Sammel-Nr. 19 51 51
Für Fernverkehr Sammel-Nr. 19 52 31

HOTEL EXCELSIOR BERLIN

Berlin, den 16/11 1940

Sehr geehrter Herr Professor Thulin

Wir sind eben im Begriff, nach Wien zurückzufahren. Können unseren Aufenthalt in Berlin nicht länger ausdehnen, umsoweniger als Ihre Bemühung wieder [illegible] ist. Bin schon 4 Wochen in Berlin! Bitte sorgen Sie dafür, dass das Minist. f. kirchl. Angelegenheiten den Bericht des Auswärtigen Amtes bald befürwortend und [illegible] beantwortet. Das ist

41

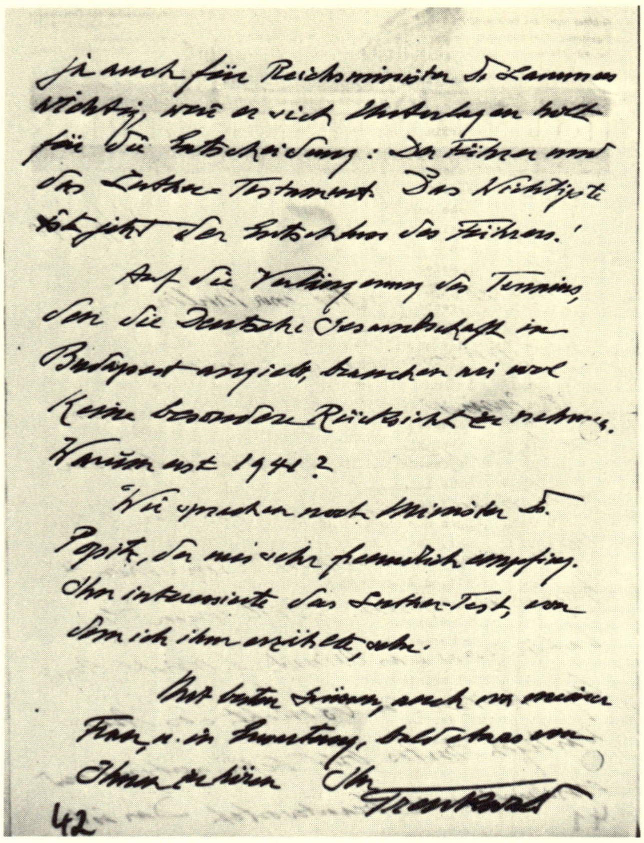
ja auch für Reichsminister Dr. Lammers wichtig, weil er sich Unterlagen holt für die Entscheidung: Der Führer und das Luther-Testament. Das Wichtigste ist jetzt der Entschluss des Führers.'

Auf die Verlängerung des Termins, den die Deutsche Gesandtschaft in Budapest [illegible], brauchen wir wol keine besondere Rücksicht zu nehmen. Warum erst 1941?

Wir sprachen noch Minister Dr. Popitz, der mich sehr freundlich empfing. Ihn interessierte das Luther-Test., von dem ich ihm erzählt habe.

Mit besten Grüssen, auch von meiner Frau, u. in Erwartung, bald etwas von Ihnen zu hören Ihr

Trenkwald

42

32–33 *H. von Trenkwald's letter to Oskar Thulin (16 November 1940)*

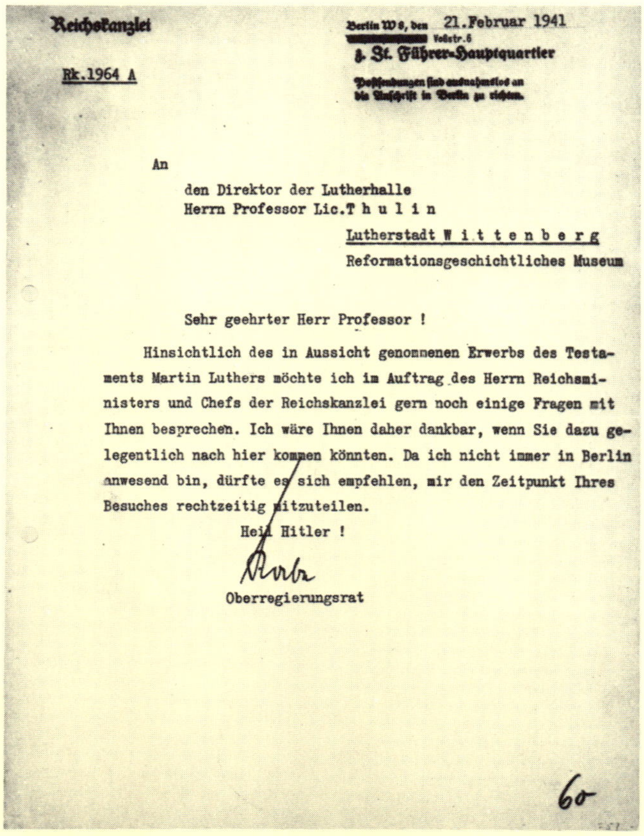
Reichskanzlei

Berlin W 8, den 21.Februar 1941
[redacted] Voßstr.6
z. Zt. Führer-Hauptquartier

Postsendungen sind ausnahmslos an die Anschrift in Berlin zu richten.

Rk.1964 A

An
den Direktor der Lutherhalle
Herrn Professor Lic.T h u l i n
Lutherstadt W i t t e n b e r g
Reformationsgeschichtliches Museum

Sehr geehrter Herr Professor !

Hinsichtlich des in Aussicht genommenen Erwerbs des Testaments Martin Luthers möchte ich im Auftrag des Herrn Reichsministers und Chefs der Reichskanzlei gern noch einige Fragen mit Ihnen besprechen. Ich wäre Ihnen daher dankbar, wenn Sie dazu gelegentlich nach hier kommen könnten. Da ich nicht immer in Berlin anwesend bin, dürfte es sich empfehlen, mir den Zeitpunkt Ihres Besuches rechtzeitig mitzuteilen.

Heil Hitler !

Kolb
Oberregierungsrat

60

34 *Letter by the German Reich Chancellery to Oskar Thulin (21 February 1941)*

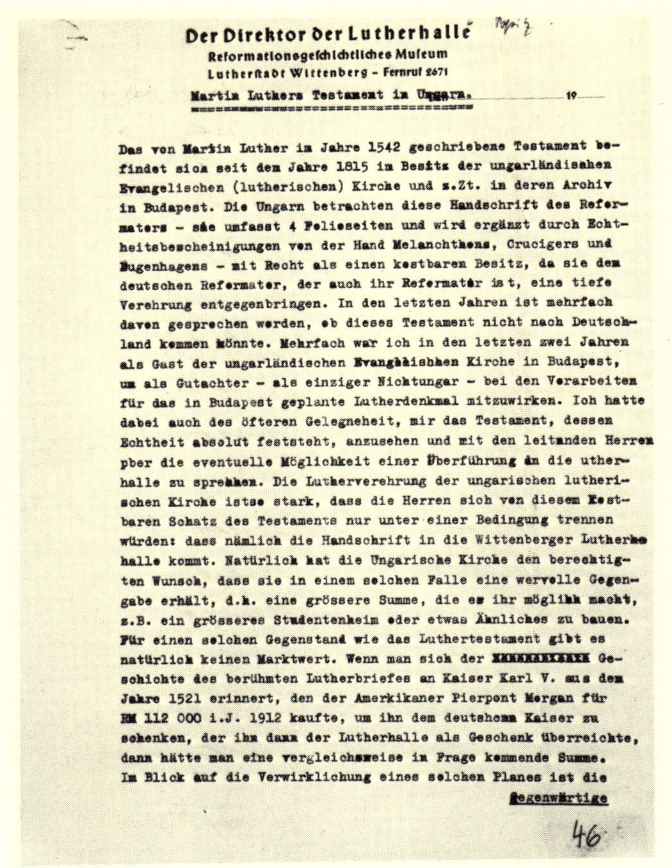

Der Direktor der Lutherhalle
Reformationsgeschichtliches Museum
Lutherstadt Wittenberg – Fernruf 2671

Martin Luthers Testament in Ungarn. 19

Das von Martin Luther im Jahre 1542 geschriebene Testament befindet sich seit dem Jahre 1815 im Besitz der ungarländischen Evangelischen (lutherischen) Kirche und z.Zt. in deren Archiv in Budapest. Die Ungarn betrachten diese Handschrift des Reformaters – sie umfasst 4 Folioseiten und wird ergänzt durch Echtheitsbescheinigungen von der Hand Melanchthons, Crucigers und Bugenhagens – mit Recht als einen kostbaren Besitz, da sie dem deutschen Reformator, der auch ihr Reformator ist, eine tiefe Verehrung entgegenbringen. In den letzten Jahren ist mehrfach davon gesprochen worden, ob dieses Testament nicht nach Deutschland kommen könnte. Mehrfach war ich in den letzten zwei Jahren als Gast der ungarländischen Evangelischen Kirche in Budapest, um als Gutachter – als einziger Nichtungar – bei den Verarbeiten für das in Budapest geplante Lutherdenkmal mitzuwirken. Ich hatte dabei auch des öfteren Gelegenheit, mir das Testament, dessen Echtheit absolut feststeht, anzusehen und mit den leitenden Herren pber die eventuelle Möglichkeit einer Überführung an die Lutherhalle zu sprechen. Die Lutherverehrung der ungarischen lutherischen Kirche istso stark, dass die Herren sich von diesem kostbaren Schatz des Testaments nur unter einer Bedingung trennen würden: dass nämlich die Handschrift in die Wittenberger Lutherhalle kommt. Natürlich hat die Ungarische Kirche den berechtigten Wunsch, dass sie in einem solchen Falle eine wervolle Gegengabe erhält, d.h. eine grössere Summe, die es ihr möglich macht, z.B. ein grösseres Studentenheim oder etwas Ähnliches zu bauen. Für einen solchen Gegenstand wie das Luthertestament gibt es natürlich keinen Marktwert. Wenn man sich der XXXXXXXXXXX Geschichte des berühmten Lutherbriefes an Kaiser Karl V. aus dem Jahre 1521 erinnert, den der Amerkikaner Pierpont Morgan für RM 112 000 i.J. 1912 kaufte, um ihn dem deutschen Kaiser zu schenken, der ihn dann der Lutherhalle als Geschenk überreichte, dann hätte man eine vergleichsweise in Frage kommende Summe. Im Blick auf die Verwirklichung eines solchen Planes ist die

Gegenwärtige

46

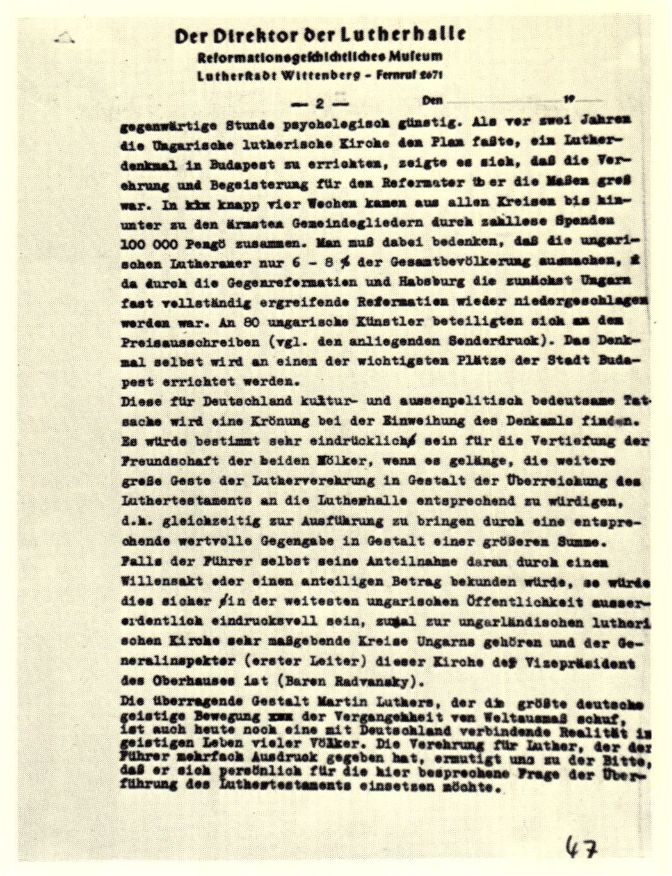

Der Direktor der Lutherhalle
Reformationsgeschichtliches Museum
Lutherstadt Wittenberg – Fernruf 2671

— 2 — Den 19

gegenwärtige Stunde psychologisch günstig. Als vor zwei Jahren die Ungarische lutherische Kirche den Plan faßte, ein Lutherdenkmal in Budapest zu errichten, zeigte es sich, daß die Verehrung und Begeisterung für den Reformator über die Maßen groß war. In kix knapp vier Wochen kamen aus allen Kreisen bis hinunter zu den ärmsten Gemeindegliedern durch zahllose Spenden 100 000 Pengö zusammen. Man muß dabei bedenken, daß die ungarischen Lutheraner nur 6 – 8 % der Gesamtbevölkerung ausmachen, da durch die Gegenreformation und Habsburg die zunächst Ungarn fast vollständig ergreifende Reformation wieder niedergeschlagen worden war. An 80 ungarische Künstler beteiligten sich an dem Preisausschreiben (vgl. den anliegenden Sonderdruck). Das Denkmal selbst wird an einem der wichtigsten Plätze der Stadt Budapest errichtet werden.
Diese für Deutschland kultur- und aussenpolitisch bedeutsame Tatsache wird eine Krönung bei der Einweihung des Denkmals finden. Es würde bestimmt sehr eindrücklich sein für die Vertiefung der Freundschaft der beiden Völker, wenn es gelänge, die weitere große Geste der Lutherverehrung in Gestalt der Überreichung des Luthertestaments an die Lutherhalle entsprechend zu würdigen, d.h. gleichzeitig zur Ausführung zu bringen durch eine entsprechende wertvolle Gegengabe in Gestalt einer größeren Summe. Falls der Führer selbst seine Anteilnahme daran durch einen Willensakt oder einen anteiligen Betrag bekunden würde, so würde dies sicher in der weitesten ungarischen Öffentlichkeit ausserordentlich eindrucksvoll sein, zumal zur ungarländischen lutherischen Kirche sehr maßgebende Kreise Ungarns gehören und der Generalinspektor (erster Leiter) dieser Kirche der Vizepräsident des Oberhauses ist (Baron Radvansky).
Die überragende Gestalt Martin Luthers, der die größte deutsche geistige Bewegung xxx der Vergangenheit von Weltausmaß schuf, ist auch heute noch eine mit Deutschland verbindende Realität im geistigen Leben vieler Völker. Die Verehrung für Luther, der der Führer mehrfach Ausdruck gegeben hat, ermutigt uns zu der Bitte, daß er sich persönlich für die hier besprochene Frage der Überführung des Luthertestaments einsetzen möchte.

47

35–36 Thulin's report on Luther's will (1941)

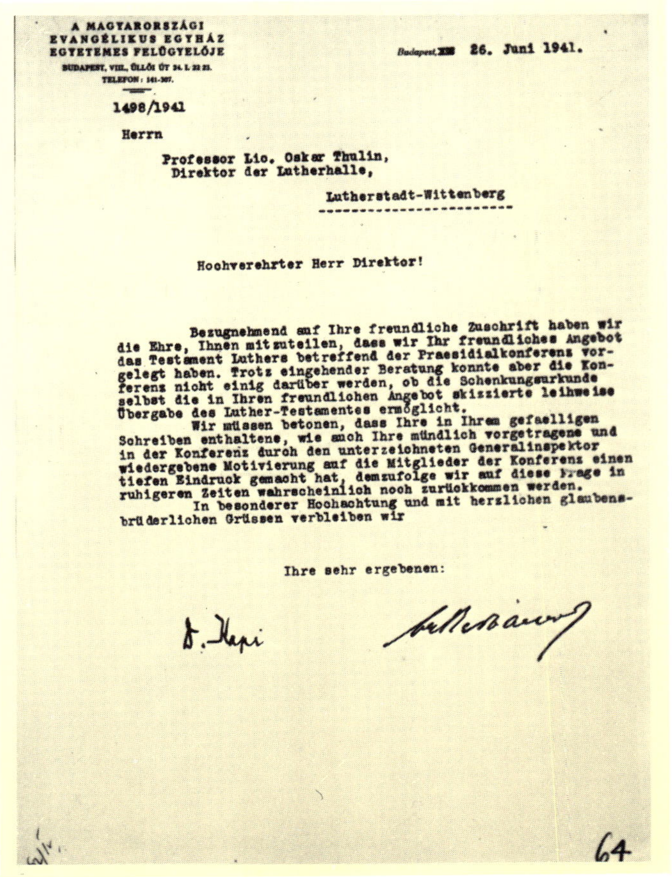

A MAGYARORSZÁGI
EVANGÉLIKUS EGYHÁZ
EGYETEMES FELÜGYELŐJE
BUDAPEST, VIII., ÜLLŐI ÚT 24. I. 22 23.
TELEFON: 141-367.

Budapest, 26. Juni 1941.

1498/1941

Herrn

Professor Lic. Oskar Thulin,
Direktor der Lutherhalle,

Lutherstadt-Wittenberg

Hochverehrter Herr Direktor!

Bezugnehmend auf Ihre freundliche Zuschrift haben wir die Ehre, Ihnen mitzuteilen, dass wir Ihr freundliches Angebot das Testament Luthers betreffend der Praesidialkonferenz vorgelegt haben. Trotz eingehender Beratung konnte aber die Konferenz nicht einig darüber werden, ob die Schenkungsurkunde selbst die in Ihren freundlichen Angebot skizzierte leihweise Übergabe des Luther-Testamentes ermöglicht.

Wir müssen betonen, dass Ihre in Ihrem gefaelligen Schreiben enthaltene, wie auch Ihre mündlich vorgetragene und in der Konferenz durch den unterzeichneten Generalinspektor wiedergebene Motivierung auf die Mitglieder der Konferenz einen tiefen Eindruck gemacht hat, demzufolge wir auf diese Frage in ruhigeren Zeiten wahrscheinlich noch zurückkommen werden.

In besonderer Hochachtung und mit herzlichen glaubensbrüderlichen Grüssen verbleiben wir

Ihre sehr ergebenen:

D. Kapi

64

37 Letter from the Presidium of the Hungarian Lutheran Church to Oskar Thulin (26 June 1941)

38 The seal with the Luther rose which the reformer received from Frederick the Wise

Bibliography

Bainton, Roland H.: *Here I Stand*. New York, 1950 (many subsequent editions)

Bainton, Roland H.: "Luther und sein Vater." In: *Luther* (Zeitschrift der Luther-Gesellschaft), 1973, No. 2.

Bainton, Roland H.: "Luther und seine Mutter." In: *Luther,* 1973, No. 3.

Benczur, László–Fabiny, Tibor et al.: *A reformáció öröksége és kötelezése* [The Heritage of the Reformation and the Duties that Derive from it]. Budapest, 1968

Berlász, Jenő: "Jankovich Miklós könyvtári gyűjteményeinek kialakulása és sorsa" [Miklós Jankovich's Book Collection and its Fate]. In: *Az Országos Széchényi Könyvtár Évkönyve,* 1970–1971. Budapest, 1971

Bœhmer, Heinrich: *Martin Luther: Road to Reformation*. New York, 1957

Bœhmer, Heinrich: "Luthers Ehe". In: *Lutherjahrbuch,* 1925

Deutsches Geschlechterbuch, 1926. Bd. 50. Görlitz, 1928

Dickens, A. G.: *Martin Luther and the Reformation*. London, 1967

Doleschall, E. A.: *Luthers Testament. Mit einer Photolitographie der Originalurkunde*. Budapest–Wien–Leipzig, 1881

Eckhardt, Karl August: *Das Lehnrecht des Sachsenspiegels*. Berlin–Frankfurt, 1956

Erikson, Erik H.: *Young Man Luther*. 1958

Fabiny, Tibor: "Luther Márton végrendelete" [Martin Luther's Will]. In: *Evangélikus Élet,* 1967, No. 64.

Fabiny, Tibor: "Originaltestament Luthers". In: *Zeichen der Zeit* (Berlin), 1967, No. 8.

Fabiny, Tibor: "Luthers Originaltestament in Ungarn." In: *Evangelische Monatshefte* (Standpunkt), 1978, No. 10.

Förstemann, K. E.: *Denkmale dem D. Martin Luther von der Hochachtung und Liebe seiner Zeitgenossen*. Nordhausen, 1846

Förstemann, K. E.: *D. Martin Luthers Testamente aus den Jahren 1537 und 1542*. Nordhausen, 1846

Friedenthal, Richard: *Luther. His Life and Times*. New York, 1970

Friedenthal, Richard: "Das evangelische Pfarrhaus im deutschen Kulturleben." In: *Luther,* 1971. No. 1.

Grisar, Hartmann, S. J.: *Luther*. Freiburg, 1924

Gyapay, Gábor: "Luther Márton végrendelete a Magyarországi Evangélikus Egyház tulajdonában van" [Martin Luther's Will is Held by the Lutheran Church of Hungary]. In: *Evangélikus Élet,* 1959, No. 8.

Gyöngyösi, Vilmos: "Dr. Luther Márton végrendelete" [Dr Martin Luther's Will]. In: *Új Harangszó,* 10 February 1946
Győry, Vilmos: "Luther Márton végrendelete" [Martin Luther's Will]. In: *Pesti Hírlap,* 28 September 1879
Három História Luther Mártonról [Three Stories about Martin Luther]. (Manuscript). Manuscript Collection of the National Széchényi Library, Budapest, Quart. Hung. 107, Oct. Hung. 372.
Harnack, Adolf von: *Martin Luther und die Grundlegung der Reformation.* Berlin, 1917
Hirschfeld, Georg von: *Die Beziehungen Luthers und seiner Gemahlin, Katharina v. Bora, zur Familie Hirschfeld.* Leipzig, 1883
Huber, Heinz–Müller, Artur: *Das Dritte Reich. Seine Geschichte in Bildern und Dokumenten.* München–Wien–Basel, 1964
Kirsch, Peter Anton: *Melanchthon's Brief an Camerarius über Luthers Heirat vom 16. Juni 1525.* Mainz, 1900
Koppen, Luise: *Katharina von Bora, Luthers Frau.* Bielefeld bei Leipzig, 1917
Köstlin, Julius–Kawerau, Gustav: *Martin Luther. Sein Leben und seine Schriften.* Berlin, 1903
Kroker, Ernst: *Katharina von Bora, Martin Luthers Frau.* Berlin, 1974
Leipziger Illustrierte Zeitung, 30 October 1880
Lilje, Hanns: *Martin Luther in Selbstzeugnissen und Bilddokumenten.* Rohwolt, 1976
Loewenich, Walter von: "Luthers Heirat". In: *Luther,* 1976, No. 2.
Ludolphy, Ingetraut: "Katharina von Bora, die 'Gehilfin' Martin Luthers". In: *Luther,* 1961. No. 2.
Luther, Martin: *Sermon von dem ehelichen Stand* (1519)
Luther, Martin: *De votis monasticis* (1521)
Luther, Martin: *Vom ehelichen Leben* (1522)
Luther, Martin: *Ursache und Antwort, dass Jungfrauen Klöster göttlich verlassen mögen* (1523)
Luther, Martin: *Ein Traubüchlein für die einfältigen Pfarrherrn* (1529)
Luther, Martin: *Von Ehesachen* (1530)
M. Luthers Werke. Tischreden. Vol. 9, Weimar, 1941
M. Luther, dargestellt von seinen Freunden und Zeitgenossen J. Mathesius, Ph. Melanchthon, L. Cranach d. Ä., Hans Sachs, u.a. Berlin, 1933
Luther's Works, American Edition. Ed. by Jaroslav Pelikan and Hartmut T. Lehman. Philadelphia, 1955 ff. 55 vols.
Masznyik, Endre: *Luther egyházszervező iratai* [Luther's Writings on Church Organization]. Vol. 6, Budapest, 1914
Mayer, Joh. Friedrich: *Dessertatio de Catharina Lutheri conjuge,* Respondente M. Richey. Hamburg, 1698
Meurer, Th. Moritz: *Katharina Luther geb. von Bora.* Leipzig, 1873
Muncz, Frigyes: "Luther végrendelete" [Luther's Will]. In: *Evangélikus Élet,* 1950, No. 44.
Mühlhaupt, Erwin: "Luthers Kampf mit der Krankheit". In: *Luther,* 1958, No. 3.
Payr, Sándor: "Luther saját kezű végrendelete" [Luther's Holograph Will]. In: *Evangélikus Egyházi Élet,* 1917, No. 48–49.
Ránki, György–Pamlényi, Ervin–Tilkovszky, Lóránd–Juhász, Gyula: *A Wil-*

helmstrasse és Magyarország. Német diplomáciai iratok Magyarországról 1933–44 [The Wilhelmstrasse and Hungary. German Foreign Office Papers on Hungary 1933–44]. Budapest, 1968
Repkow, Eike von: *Der Sachsenspiegel.* In unsere heutige Muttersprache übertragen von H. Ch. Hirsch. Leipzig, 1936
Richter, David: *Genealogia Lutherorum, oder historische Erzählung von D. Mart. Lutheri.* Berlin–Leipzig, 1733
Ritter, Johann, Ludwig (Hrg.): *Feyer des dritten Jubelfestes in Zöllsdorf.* Leipzig, 1817
Rumy, Karl: "Catharina von Bora, Dr. Martin Luthers Gattin, wahrscheinlich eine geborene Magyarin". In: *Pressburger Aehrenlese zur Belehrung und Unterhaltung,* 1831, No. 43.
Rünssberg, Eberhard von: *Der Sachsenspiegel. Bilder aus der Heidelberger Handschrift.* Leipzig, 1961
Scheel, Otto: *Dokumente zu Luthers Entwicklung.* Tübingen, 1929
Schubert, Christoph: *Die Berichte über Luthers Tod und Begräbnis.* Weimar, 1917
Schumann, Wolfgang–Hass, Gerhart: *Deutschland im zweiten Weltkrieg.* Berlin, 1974
Schwiebert, E. G.: *Luther and his Times.* St. Louis, 1950
Seeberg, Reinhold: "Luthers Anschauung von dem Geschlechtsleben und der Ehe und ihre geschichtliche Stellung". In: *Lutherjahrbuch,* 1925
Seidemann, J. C.: "Luthers Grundbesitz". In: *Zeitschrift für historische Theologie,* 1860, No. IV.
Shirer, William L.: *The Rise and Fall of the Third Reich. A History of Nazi Germany.* London, 1962
Sólyom, Jenő: *Luther és Magyarország* [Luther and Hungary]. Budapest, 1933
Sólyom, Jenő: "Luther Márton saját kezűleg írt végrendeletéről" [On Martin Luther's Holograph Will]. In: *Evangélikus Élet,* 1964, No. 12.
Varsányi, Mátyás: *Isten embere. Dr. Luther Márton élete* [Man of God. A Life of Dr. Martin Luther]. Budapest, 1938
Vető, Lajos: *Vom Aufbau der Kirche in Ungarn.* Leipzig, 1955
Wiczián, Dezső: "Az elfelejtett testamentum" [The Forgotten Will]. In: *Keresztyén Igazság,* 1937, No. 10.
Wiener genealogisches Taschenbuch 1927/28. Bd. 2. Wien, 1928
Zarncke, Lilly: "Der Begriff der Liebe in Luthers Äusserungen über die Ehe". In: *Theologische Blätter,* 1931, No. 45–49.

Printed in Hungary, 1984
Kner Printing House, Dürer Workshop, Békéscsaba